Love in the Key of Three

Love in the Key of Three

The Trinitarian Theology of Wm. Paul Young

ANDREW CHRISTIAN NELSON

WIPF & STOCK · Eugene, Oregon

LOVE IN THE KEY OF THREE
The Trinitarian Theology of Wm. Paul Young

Copyright © 2022 Andrew Christian Nelson. All rights reserved. Except for brief quotations in critical publications or reviews, no part of this book may be reproduced in any manner without prior written permission from the publisher. Write: Permissions, Wipf and Stock Publishers, 199 W. 8th Ave., Suite 3, Eugene, OR 97401.

Wipf & Stock
An Imprint of Wipf and Stock Publishers
199 W. 8th Ave., Suite 3
Eugene, OR 97401

www.wipfandstock.com

PAPERBACK ISBN: 978-1-6667-1547-7
HARDCOVER ISBN: 978-1-6667-1548-4
EBOOK ISBN: 978-1-6667-1549-1

MARCH 1, 2022 9:10 AM

Scripture quotations marked as originating from "ESV" are from ESV® Bible (The Holy Bible, English Standard Version®), copyright © 2001 by Crossway, a publishing ministry of Good News Publishers. Used by permission. All rights reserved.

Scripture quotations marked (NIV) are taken from the Holy Bible, New International Version®, NIV®. Copyright © 1973, 1978, 1984, 2011 by Biblica, Inc.™ Used by permission of Zondervan. All rights reserved worldwide. www.zondervan.comThe "NIV" and "New International Version" are trademarks registered in the United States Patent and Trademark Office by Biblica, Inc.™

Scripture quotations taken from the (NASB®) New American Standard Bible®, Copyright © 1960, 1971, 1977, 1995, 2020 by The Lockman Foundation. Used by permission. All rights reserved. www.lockman.org.

Scripture quotations marked NLT are taken from the Holy Bible, New Living Translation, Copyrigth © 1996, 2004, 2015 by Tyndale House Foundation. Used by permission of Tyndale House Publishers, Inc., Carol Stream, Illinois 60188. All rights reserved.

For Finley Indiana

"The LORD your God is in your midst, a mighty one who will save; he will rejoice over you with gladness; *he will quiet you by his love*..."

ZEPHANIAH 3:17, ESV (EMPHASIS MINE)

Contents

Acknowledgments | ix

Introduction | xi

PART 1
A Love in the Key of Three: The Triune Community

Chapter 1 Enraptured Relation:
The Shared Love of the Trinity | 3

Chapter 2 The God Who Submits | 10

Chapter 3 The God Without a Religion | 26

Chapter 4 The God Who is Light | 36

Chapter 5 The God Who Wants to Be Known:
Encountering Young's Mysticism | 47

PART 2
When Love Meets the Broken: The Healing Work of God

Chapter 6 The Condition of Humanity | 59

Chapter 7 Atoning Love | 70

Chapter 8 Hell and Hope | 82

Appendix   Addressing James B. De Young and Common Misconceptions of Young's Theology | 97

AFTERWORD | 124

Bibliography | 125

Acknowledgments

To the living subject of this book, Wm. Paul Young: you are a conversation starter. That's about the best compliment I can give you regarding your writing and something tells me that you will receive it gratefully. I so appreciate your willingness to go to the "deep end" of the pool and reveal to others what you find there. Your work makes being a theologian fun and exciting. Thank you for your contribution to the conversation about God's goodness and for your eagerness to love.

To my family: Kristi, Isla and Finley. I really don't have words to describe what you mean to me, and to our Father. Kristi you are the best mother our children could ask for, and the only partner in crime I need; Isla, you will nourish this world with color; and Finley, you will purify it with the flaming fire of God's love.

To my in-laws, Barb and Mike: God is madly in love with you. I hope you know that. Thank you for loving my children so well, and for being such a big help to us as we raise them.

To my Dad: Thank you for always being a presence in my life and for all of those early mornings spent praying in front of the high school. I won't forget them.

Acknowledgments

To Prof. Tom Greggs: Thank you for your support during the process of earning my doctorate. This book is largely the result of your faithful and persistent guidance.

To my best friends and my counsel: Jeremy, Kevin, Drew, and Ralph. You guys make living this life easier. I'm better because of you in so many ways.

To the voices from my past: Benny, Raleigh, Tim, Donna, Dottie, Art, Rob, Jack, and so many others. Your support, smiles, and hugs in critical times during my life kept me alive.

Introduction

THEOLOGY, IN ITS PUREST AND most worthwhile form, seeks to offer careful considerations about God and God's creation. It is, in its multitude of facets, the journey towards knowing the truth about God in a more full and comprehensive sense to the end that the believer in God may have a clearer understanding of supernatural truth, truth that flows out of Heaven and into our world. This deeper understanding of God's truth then leads people further out of the darkness of their minds, and into the wonderful light that is God's essential being. As theologian Tom Greggs says, theology is the journey of renewing the mind, the journey of Romans 12:2.[1] It is the journey of leaving behind the lies which have so torn our hearts asunder and pillaged our humanity and threatened our divine purpose. It is the embracing of the Son of Man, in all of his humble glory, the proverbial jump from the cliff of distrust into the refreshing waters of endless grace.

Because theology is scientific in nature, it requires processes for trying to discern this supernatural truth of God. We set up frameworks and systems that help us to better read and understand Scripture, bringing us to encounter the historical context of that which was written, while trying to discern God's intended meaning with the text. In this journey of theology, however, there

---

1. "And do not be conformed to this world, but be transformed by the renewing of your mind, so that you may prove what the will of God is, that which is good and acceptable and perfect" Romans 12:2 (NASB). See Tom Greggs, "Task and Method of Theology," 318.

Introduction

is the risk of process replacing that which breathes infinite meaning into life: encounter. We humans are designed for encounter with God. I do not necessarily speak of experience when I refer to encounter though an encounter with God could result in feelings or the excitement of our senses. I mean coming face-to-face with the triune God of love, not only seeing how his love has invaded and permeated every corner of cosmic existence, but our own personal stories. Encounter is meeting God, as he meets us, in the garden of our own souls. When this encounter is the result of our theology, or the goal of our theology, then this scientific process of theology transforms from black and white into endless dimensions of cascading color. Some theologians point to encounter with God by providing answers to difficult questions and we desperately need these people. Wm. Paul Young, however, creates a space for conversation with God through asking poignant questions about reality.

Young is the author of six books, three fiction works (*The Shack, Cross Roads, and Eve*), two devotionals (*The Shack Reflections, Cross Roads Reflections*) and a sixth which acts as a non–fiction conversation-starter for important theological issues (*Lies We Believe about God*). In these works of Young's, relational encounter with God is expressed in such a way as to not only challenge our preconceptions of what theology is or should be, but precisely what relationship with God ought to look like. We see God, not merely as the desired goal of an intellectual pursuit, but as primarily a triune community who invites humanity into relationship with itself. This relationship, for Young, is the goal of theology as well as the end result of the process. But it is more than this. For Young, relationship with God *is* the theological journey, and every person, regardless of whether they know it or not, is on this journey towards a deeper encounter with God. And God, fueled by his approachable yet infinitely complex love, is on this journey towards us, travelling down, as Jesus says in *The Shack*, "any road" present in our lives to find us.[2] This is the journey that Young invites his readers on: encounter.

2. Young, *Shack*, 182.

Introduction

It is because of this blend of theology and encounter with the Trinity in Young's works, this union of pastoral considerations and an intellectual pursuit of truth, that I set out to write what is, at the very least, designed to be foundational primer for understanding Young's often misunderstood theology.[3] This blending of relational encounter with God with the pursuit of truth has miraculously made theologians out of each of his millions upon millions of readers, often without their knowing. This reveals that Young has the rare gift of writing in such a way as to invite believers in Jesus, and unbelievers, onto the very same journey of discovering the God of love in their midst. For this reason, his work deserves to be discovered and explored. This work is an encounter of sorts with Young's thinking: it is a presentation of his beliefs which are perceived by this author to be critical to the ongoing conversation about God's grace and nature.

Love in the Key of Three is intended to be a comprehensive exploration of Young's theology. However, *comprehensive* does not mean *exhaustive* in its treatment of Young's beliefs: there will undoubtedly be some corner(s) left intentionally or unintentionally unexplored. Effort will also not be exerted to trace theological themes across all of Young's platforms. In many cases, themes are only focused on in one or a few sources. The reason for this being that Young is consistent in his presentation of his convictions and therefore there is no need to bring an onslaught of sources in just to prove a point into a coma. This work is meant to be a map of sorts, a guide for fans of Young's works who simply desire to better explore his beliefs for their own pursuit of truth, and for academics interested in Young's trinitarian theology and the parallels between his beliefs and those of other theologians both classical and more modern. I've studied Young for quite some time, not only as a casual reader of his books but also as an academic. Consequently, this is the result of years of study and contains my own analysis

---

3. While the misunderstandings will be addressed in the main chapters of the book, the appendix will have a clear presentation of many of these misunderstandings mostly using the works of James B. De Young to frame the discussion.

Introduction

and observations of his works. I do not purport to be correct on all my observations. However, I do take care to cite the sources which have led to my observations and conclusions about Young's work so that my argument can be clear for the purposes of conversation. Thus, my arguments are made to the best of my ability. Yet, a challenge exists in analyzing Young's theology, especially in his fiction works, to which I may have fallen victim at times (the reader will have to decide). In Young's works of fiction, how do we determine what is meant to be divine truth communicated to the reader, and what is simply plot for the sake of advancing the story? This is an important hurdle to overcome and an issue deserving of a strategy to overcome it.

Essentially, this work is an exploration not just of his fiction, and non-fiction books, but also his many sermons, interviews, and articles. Therefore, it is worth noting that the themes which are argued to exist in his fiction, are also largely expressed in either his non-fiction, or his sermons and interviews. This helps to establish what theologians call his "operant theology" or the theology which is "embedded" within his practices as a Christian and theologian.[4] These practices are argued to be inherently theological, for as Bhatti et al. state, "Christian practice is, itself, 'faith seeking understanding.'"[5] What readers encounter in Young's works is the outworking of his own faith, a faith which is presented as a journey towards a deeper understanding of the Father, Son, and Spirit.[6] Another basis from which we will explore Young's fiction is found in the work of Robert Paul Roth. Roth believes that story is a vessel through which the message of God can be communicated to the world.[7] Roth argues that this reality is seen in the gospels which communicate often fantastical elements that Christians accept as true even if the events go against what is presumably possible in

---

4. See Bhatti et al., *God in Practice*, 54.

5. Bhatti et al., *God in Practice*, 53.

6. This is not to say that I will cross-reference every theological point with another form of media. This only suggests that the truth he communicates in his fiction can also be found in other media types.

7. Roth, *Story and Reality*, 30.

Introduction

life.[8] Young's fiction works, therefore, are assumed to be stories, but stories with theological messages due to their subject matter. These works are considered "theological fiction" and as such communicate truth embedded with story. Therefore, this book assumes that story can communicate truth, and often communicates truth using imagery.[9] A final basis used for the exploration of Young's theology is the presence of overt theological convictions within Young's writings. Young is very concerned with presenting both God and humanity as accurately as possible. Whenever Young is representing God in some manner, I have assumed that he is intending to communicate a theological conviction he holds about God. Likewise, whenever Young is presenting some aspect of humanity, I have assumed that he is communicating a theological conviction about humanity. However, because Young is not writing as a systematic theologian, these statements ought not be seen as exhaustive representations of his beliefs. Young is presenting his beliefs about God, but he is doing so in a very particular genre, using imagery. Images, as Papa declares in *The Shack*, never fully represent the nature of God. However, they can be helpful in expressing truths about him.[10] His statements are not exhaustive and should not be treated as such: they are images that express truth. Because these are not comprehensive statements, there is room for error in assessing his positions. My hope is that these guidelines will act to minimize any error at least enough to provide healthy foundations for conversation. These interpretive guidelines, when combined, form the basis for the methodology I use for interpreting Young's fiction while being mindful to not

---

8. Roth, *Story and Reality*, 30.

9. See Young, *Cross Roads*, 286. Imagery is a consistent tool Young uses to express theological truths through story. This is affirmed in *Cross Roads* when Grandmother says that God uses imagery for communication of himself to humanity. In the story, she was referring to the Father's decision to manifest as a little girl during an interaction with Tony. The little girl expresses the childlike love and trust that Young affirms exists in the Father.

10. See Young, *The Shack*, 93, where Young, through Papa, seems to be addressing his readers on this very topic. God appears to Mack as a female, and later a male, to express, metaphorically, what God is like.

Introduction

be overly intellectual so as to alienate readers, or to neglect the importance of encounter in Young's works.

In order to create this balance between intellectual pursuit and encounter with God, this book is designed to be both pastorally sensitive and intellectually challenging, trying to express the same blend of relationship and intellectual pursuit expressed by Young in his works. To accomplish this goal, the work is divided into two primary sections, each designed to explore an aspect of Young's trinitarian theology with a view to demonstrate how his theology is designed to impact relationship with God. Part 1, "A Love in the Key of Three: The Triune Community," is focused on interacting with how Young portrays the nature of the Trinity in its interrelationship with itself, as well as God's actions towards humanity and how these actions further reveal his nature. Part 2, "When Love Meets the Broken: The Healing Work of God," is focused primarily on Young's soteriology (theology of salvation). The Trinity's role in redeeming humanity is explored as is the role of humanity's participation in salvation.

Each chapter is divided into three sections. The first section is an overview of Young's beliefs about a given topic; the second is a comparison between Young and theologian(s) I've deemed contain important continuity with Young; and finally, a section called "Encountering Young" where I try to discern the overt biblical foundations for Young's beliefs, at least as I perceive them. This third section is my own effort to discern precisely where in Scripture Young's beliefs might be represented. Because this section is my own personal analysis, great care is taken to ensure that I am not proof-texting Scripture or Young's works to establish parallels. I am merely using my own background in biblical interpretation to establish whether I see these themes in Scripture, or not. After the two main parts is an appendix addressing what I perceive to be common misconceptions regarding Young's theology.

The content in this work will reveal that Young's theology, in many ways, is hemmed in by question marks. The questions he asks about God and humanity have a way of penetrating into the innermost recesses of all that it means to be a Christian, and in

Introduction

some respects, creating more questions (this is especially the case with his understanding of hell and judgment). But Young does not seem concerned with having certainty about all truths related to God. The truth is often in the questions themselves, and the journey towards the answers to these questions. As Tony says in *Cross Roads*, "What if it's not about getting anywhere?"[11] Indeed, Young seems to ask his readers, what if the journey with God *is* the answer to life's most precious questions? This work will interact with questions asked by Young, and perhaps create more questions for the reader. But that is the difference between merely intellectual theology and encounter with the triune God. God, in Young's mind, is not so concerned with our having certainty. He wants us, the whole of us, in every moment, to consciously participate with him on our own journey. We are, each of us, travelling down our own Damascus roads, letting Jesus remove the scales from our eyes. I'm convinced Young's theology is a beautiful tool for that journey.

11. Young, *Cross Roads*, 34.

Introduction

PART 1

A LOVE IN THE KEY OF THREE
The Triune Community

"If God has ever been alone, there would be neither a basis in the universe for love nor a framework for relationship."

YOUNG, *LIES WE BELIEVE ABOUT GOD*, 239

CHAPTER 1

ENRAPTURED RELATION
The Shared Love of the Trinity

MAKING THE DECLARATIVE STATEMENT THAT "God is love" is commonplace in Christianity. Chances are, if we've been inside of a church, we've at least seen a banner with the phrase. On one of the main roads where I used to live in Sparks, Nevada, there is a church banner with a letter from God that reads "I love you," and then has God's signature. When I see this, or t-shirts with similar branding, I always wonder whether we feel that we must have this signage or clothing because, deep down, we feel disconnected from God's love and are trying to make it more tangible to ourselves and others. Perhaps we are even trying to define it in some way. The phrase "God is love," like the phrase "God loves you," does not have definition apart from an understanding of who this God is in his personhood. Without an understanding of God, the phrase is simply disconnected and lonely. If God is a singular entity, for example, then we cannot understand how this singular being embodies love and expresses love because there is no object of love, at least until one is created. Love, therefore, would not be

A Love in the Key of Three: The Triune Community

witnessed independently of the creature and could be concluded to be non-existent before creation.

In the case of the trinitarian God, this embodiment of love comes from a God who is triune in his essential nature: one being, three persons. The God of the Bible, the God whom Jesus revealed (John 1), is paradoxically three persons, and yet one person. Such a statement makes little sense from a naturalistic perspective, for how can three beings also be one?[1] After all, how can 1+1+1=1? C.S. Lewis comments on this reality in *Mere Christianity*:

> Now the Christian account of God involves just the same principle. The human level is a simple and rather empty level. On the human level one person is one being, and any two persons are two separate beings–just as, in two dimensions (say on a flat sheet of paper) one square is one figure, and any two squares are two separate figures. On the Divine level you still find personalities; but up there you find them combined in new ways which we, who do not live on that level, cannot imagine. In God's dimension, so to speak, you find a being who is three Persons while remaining one Being, just as a cube is six squares while remaining one cube.[2]

A God who exists as a single entity, while perhaps containing some similar characteristics to the biblical God, would seem to arise from what Lewis calls a human account of God. It is not difficult for a human to imagine a being who is singular and yet has loving characteristics. Yet, the God revealed by Jesus is quite foreign to a human account. He is one being, three persons, and *they* are love.

For Young, to say that God is love, is to say that God has always been in a community, with each member of the Trinity acting in self-sacrificial love towards the other. For Young, there can be no declarative statement that "God is love" without the triune existence of God as Father, Son, and Spirit living

---

1. Naturalism is here defined as the philosophical belief that everything in existence is created, and lives, because of natural causes instead of supernatural.

2. Lewis, *Mere Christianity*, 162.

Enraptured Relation

"face-to-face-to-face" with one another in community.³ Love cannot find expression apart from relationship. Divine love, therefore, cannot exist without the relationship of one member of the Trinity to another. Each member of the Trinity loves the other fully and completely, and love is defined by this selfless focus on the other member.

This foundational concept runs through Young's works. In *Eve*, the central character Lilly witnesses the creation of the universe. After seeing the void which existed before creation, a "detonation" occurs, sending "energy" and "information" into the void.⁴ After this event, a "tidal surge of voices rose, engulfing her [Lilly] in an assembly of scents. Sweet incense became a ballad of yearning, a choreographed dance of being and belonging. Around and around through it all rippled not One, not Two, but Three Voices– and yet only One. A magnificent laugh of raucous affection."⁵ The description of creation in *Eve* illustrates the beauty that triune unity and "affection" bring to creation, even going so far as to state that all creation comes from this community. Indeed, in *Eve*, we see that there is no loving existence of God independent of community.

In *Cross Roads*, Young also presents God as an eternal community. When the main character, Tony, meets Jesus, Tony at first perceives him to be alone because he meets him "in the middle of nowhere," a location that is a part of his soul.⁶ Tony asks Jesus if he likes living alone and Jesus responds, "Don't know. I've never lived alone."⁷ God's communal nature is also seen in a statement which finds a parallel to the account of creation in *Eve*. Jesus tells Tony that Tony was created "by a community to exist in community."⁸

---

3. Young, *Lies*, 239.
4. Young, *Eve*, 15.
5. Young, *Eve*, 15 and 16. Young's description of creation has some thematic elements in common with Tolkien's account of creation in *Silmarillion*. See Tolkien, *Silmarillion*, 3–5.
6. Young, *Cross Roads*, 56.
7. Young, *Cross Roads*, 56.
8. Young, *Cross Roads*, 56.

A Love in the Key of Three: The Triune Community

That this creating community is one of interdependent trust and love is seen in Jesus's trust of Papa's plans for Tony, plans that Jesus himself does not yet know. Jesus trusts that Papa has a reason for not telling him the plans, and suspects this reason is that Papa knows that Jesus likes surprises.[9] It is subtle, affectionate undertones such as these, that help to form Young's trinitarian theology. He not only states, intellectually, that God is one being, three persons, but also offers an idea of what this being acts like if he is indeed love.

The communal nature of God is also seen in *The Shack*. When Mack first comes in contact with the Trinity, Papa embraces him and says, "My, my, my, how I do love you!"[10] Mack is then introduced to Jesus, and Sarayu, the Holy Spirit manifested as an Asian woman. When Mack asks which one of the three figures is God, they respond in unison, "I am."[11] The implication in this, and many other parts of the book, is that the Trinity is united in love for Mack. Their community, therefore, is one of unified expression of love, and Papa tells Mack that he has always been "Smack dab in the center" of this love.[12] Because God is a community of love, this love, by nature, seeks to be given to humanity. This realization is key to Mack's journey of healing from the Great Sadness, and central to Young's overarching theological framework.

In situating his theology atop the pre-existent love and community of the Trinity, Young makes a subtle yet critical statement about God: the nature of the Trinity existed independently of human action. This is a way of viewing God in a type of theological vacuum and implies that God will always be love towards humanity because this love existed *independently* of humanity, and is not impacted by humanity. Humanity, therefore, cannot do anything to cause God to be unloving towards it. His love never ceases because it has *never* ceased thereby revealing its nature to be eternal and unending. This pre-existent, unending and eternal communal

---

9. Young, *Cross Roads*, 67.
10. Young, *Shack*, 83.
11. Young, *Shack*, 87.
12. Young, *Shack*, 98.

Enraptured Relation

love of God acts as the very seed from which springs all other aspects of Young's theology. Each emphasis of Young's is directly connected to, and informed by, his view of trinitarian love.

COMPARING YOUNG AND T.F. TORRANCE'S TRINITARIAN THEOLOGY

Young's emphasis on trinitarian community finds great parallel with the trinitarian theology of T.F. Torrance. In order to understand the concept of the communal love of the Trinity in Torrance's theology, his use of the Greek term *perichoresis* must be explored briefly. As Torrance notes, the term likely originates in the writings of St. Gregory of Nazianzus and was used by St. Gregory to explain the interrelationship of the human and divine side of Christ.[13] Torrance observes that *perichoresis* derives from *chora*, the Greek word for "space" or "room," or from *chorein* meaning "to contain," "to make room," or "to go forward."[14] Torrance argues that it indicates a "mutual containing or enveloping of realities" or "coindwelling."[15] For Gregory, this was a statement regarding the mutual dwelling of Christ's human side and divine side within his person.[16] Yet, the term was then used to describe the relationship between the Father, Son, and Spirit. According to Torrance, the Father, Son, and Spirit are in a co-indwelling existence: "The three divine Persons mutually dwell in one another and coinhere or in-exist in one another while nevertheless remaining other than one another and distinct from one another."[17] This existence of God is eternal in nature and is only revealed to humanity through the person of Jesus Christ.[18] Jesus Christ, in his incarnation, reveals

---

13. Torrance, *Doctrine of God*, 102.
14. Torrance, *Doctrine of God*, 102.
15. Torrance, *Doctrine of God*, 102.
16. See St. Gregory of Nazianzus, *God and Christ*, especially Oration 4, 93–116.
17. Torrance, *Doctrine of God*, 102.
18. Torrance's emphasis has parallels to St. Gregory's description of the Trinity as having a "supra-temporal" existence, an existence outside of time.

this eternal nature of God in what Torrance calls "our spatio-temporal" existence, or humanity's life within *space* and *time*.[19] Jesus connects humanity to God, and God to humanity, in the power of the Holy Spirit, thereby restoring an intimacy between the triune God and humanity.[20] Torrance argues that we do not know "the Father except as the Father of the Son, and do not know the Son except as the Son of the Father, and do not know the Holy Spirit except as the Spirit of the Father and of the Son."[21] In short, God cannot be known as a singular entity. Each member of the Godhead is dependent on the other, and expresses the nature of the other, while retaining its own unique personhood. Torrance famously says that "What God is toward us in his saving condescension to be with us in Jesus Christ, he is in himself, and what he is in his real presence with us and in us as the Holy Spirit, he is in himself."[22] Therefore, when Torrance affirms that the incarnation reveals the eternal love and grace of God (the love and grace of God that has always existed within the Trinity),[23] he means to reveal precisely the same principle expressed by Young in his works: God has always been in a community of love, and because of his nature as grace and love, longs to invite humanity into relationship with himself. This is the essence of what we see of God's nature in Young's works.

ENCOUNTERING YOUNG

Though much of Young's understanding of the Trinity is expressed in fiction without overt reference to Scripture, the heart

---

See St. Gregory, *God and Christ*, 71.

19. Torrance, *Doctrine of God*, 95.

20. This is covered extensively in Torrance's *Incarnation and Atonement*.

21. Torrance, *Doctrine of God*, 92. This principle is reflected throughout The Gospel of John. See especially John 5:19-27, John 10, and John 17. Jesus's language establishes the intimate connection between himself and his Father, both in identity and in action.

22. Torrance, *Doctrine of God*, 92.

23. Torrance, *Doctrine of God*, 90.

Enraptured Relation

of what Young is saying is firmly rooted in the Bible. From the beginning we see that God is not a singular being. We see this in Gen 1:26 where God is said to make "man in our image, after our likeness" (KJV). We also see explicit language speaking of the trinitarian nature of God throughout the New Testament (see John 17:11, Luke 9:35, Matt 29:19, and Gal 4:6). Scripture is very clear indeed: Jesus came to reveal the heart, not of a singular God, but of a triune God (John 1).

Young then combines this scriptural notion of God's triune existence with the notion that God is love (1 John 4:8), a statement that is distinctly New Testament in nature. In the Old Testament, God was portrayed as loving along with a myriad of other attributes. Yet, in the New Testament, John the beloved apostle, reveals that God *is* love. Young expresses what this love must look like in the existence of a triune relationship. Love, if originating from God, must be communal in nature. Young's work is especially helpful in expressing, at least in part, what this love must look like. Love is defined by the apostle Paul as containing excellent characteristics such as patience, kindness, forgiveness and many others (1 Cor 13:4–6). Furthermore, the fruits of the Spirit as described in Gal 5:22–23 contain elements that are distinctive attributes of love: "joy, peace, longsuffering, gentleness" in addition to others (KJV). God, therefore, is love and love looks a certain way. Furthermore, love does not look like the opposite of its characteristics: love is not impatient, harsh, or lacking joy. God, therefore, is not these things. God is love and this love is inherently communal and expressive of these characteristics.

The importance of the trinitarian community in Young's theology will be established throughout this work. Young's understandings of every aspect of God's nature; Christ's atoning work; the state of humanity; and eternal judgement is informed by the shared love of the Trinity. If a concept violates this love, then it is not truth, according to Young. For Young, the Trinity is engaged in an eternal love affair, a dance, which expresses a symphony so beautiful and transcendent that it can only be described as existing in an otherworldly key, the *key* of trinitarian love.

CHAPTER 2

The God Who Submits

For Young, there is no understanding of divine love apart from an understanding of submission: saying that God is love is to say that God lives in submission, not only to Godself, but to humanity. The central conversation point that often ignites the wildfire of dialogue surrounding this topic is the notion that God is, at his core, a God of submissive love.[1] This concept of the Trinity living in a submissive relationship, not only to one another, but also to humanity, is often difficult to process. I suspect this is the case because of our desiring to maintain God's position on the throne of the universe: God is all-powerful and mighty. The idea that God submits seemingly challenges this concept especially when our view of leadership, or kingship, is one based on the exertion of force or authority. Yet, for Young, submission is the expression not only of the *agape* love of God but also of God's power. God lives in a submissive existence within the triune community, and also humanity. Without this submission, there is no genuine servitude and consequently no love.

---

1. I do not use the term "wildfire" lightly. Young was a guest lecturer in one of my classes at Nevada Christian College (formerly Multnomah University Nevada) and his presentation ignited passionate conversation with my students for two weeks.

The God Who Submits

Young maintains that God is not in the business of controlling his creation. He states that "love and relationship trump control every time."[2] For Young, control is associated with the exertion of authority and dominance.[3] This authority, dominance, and control, does not originate with God and is the antithesis of submissive love. Submission, however, does originate with God.[4] Submission has always existed within the eternal Godhead.[5] This submissive love is precisely the way in which God relates to humanity. God created humanity in order to love it through relational servitude. He created humanity to partake in the eternal love affair of the Father, Son, and Spirit. He created humanity to become partakers of the eternally submissive Godhead, grafted into and enveloped by the fires of God's servant nature.

Young likens the submissive relationship between the Godhead and humanity to the relationship between a parent and a child. He recalls the birth of his first child, and how this "Six pounds of humanity reduced a grown man to a weepy mush, ready to forgo usual and taken-for-granted pleasures, like sleep, in order to serve."[6] The critical element in this relationship between parent and child is the choice, or perhaps necessity, to relinquish control and dominance in favor of nurturing and love. This love is a genuine submission to the needs of the child. God chooses to submit to the needs of humanity, but also the choices humanity makes on a daily basis. For Young, to override these decisions of humanity, is to exert a sovereignty which is not conducive to a loving relationship. God submits to humanity's needs, as a parent does to a child, and to the choices humans make because he is others-centered and considers human choice to be holy ground.[7] This is not Young's way of minimizing the power of God. Rather, it is a *redefinition* of power and authority. God submits to humanity's

2. Young, *Lies*, 42.
3. Young, *Lies*, 42.
4. Young, *Lies*, 42.
5. Young, *Lies*, 47.
6. Young, *Lies*, 42.
7. Young, *Lies*, 39 and 47.

A Love in the Key of Three: The Triune Community

decisions out of respect for humanity. This is a defining element of the power of God in Young's theology. However, Young does not believe in a passive or deistic God who simply relaxes while humanity makes choices.[8] To the contrary, he believes that God, after submitting to the decisions made by humanity, "climbs into [these decisions]," including sin, and uses them for his children's ultimate good.[9] This is not to suggest that there are not consequences for poor decisions, for Young himself, in honestly presenting the consequences which arose out of his three-month long affair, does not make light of his actions.[10] However, he affirms that God does not abandon humanity to its decisions, always being "for us" in the middle of whatever chaos we create.[11] God's love, therefore, submits through the allowance of choice and also through God's service of humanity in both the redemption of the broken aspects of humanity that led to those broken decisions, and participation in decisions which are compatible with his own love.[12]

The image of "boxes" is a critical one in Young's theology. Young seems to use this imagery to describe the often-self-imposed contexts in which humanity lives. Our "boxes" are our perceptions of self and God, and really, all the identities which we adopt for ourselves.[13] A God of dominance would simply destroy the boxes and tell the individual inside to *shape-up* and *try harder*. However, Young maintains that the God who is love, who relates to humanity in perfect submission, enters these boxes making them

---

8. See Elwell, *Dictionary of Theology*, 329. Elwell admits that the term has a wide range of meaning, however, it can be used to speak of God as only acting as a "first cause" for the world, allowing the world to operate on its own after his initial creation.

9. Young, *Lies*, 48.

10. Young speaks of his affair many times. For an example, see Wm. Paul Young, "I want to be More like Oprah," https://wmpaulyoung.com/i-want-to-be-more-like-oprah-watch-interview/.

11. Young, *Lies*, 48.

12. Young's assertions seem to be a clear presentation of Rom 8:28: "And we know that for those who love God all things work together for good, for those who are called according to his purpose." (ESV)

13. Young, *Lies*, 201.

The God Who Submits

hallowed ground.[14] While God is not confined by any box built by humanity, he willingly chooses to participate with humanity in its chosen context, with its chosen beliefs and perceptions. As Young says so poignantly, "The only time we will find God in a box is because God wants to be where we are."[15] This is incarnation. This is Christ's emptying of himself. This is the self-sacrificing, other-centered love of the triune God, expressed fully as God enters our box called human life. As Young states: "What is incarnation–God becoming fully human–if not complete and utter submission to us?" God, by nature, submits.

Perhaps the most obvious example of God's submission in *The Shack* is seen in the humanity of Jesus. A striking example of Jesus's humanity is seen when Mack walks in on the Trinity just after Jesus has accidentally dropped "a large bowl of some sort of batter of sauce on the floor."[16] The Godhead is laughing at the situation, and Sarayu makes the comment that humans are clumsy.[17] Young is presenting a clear consequence of the incarnation, yet perhaps not one that is often considered. What exactly did Jesus do that was characteristic of humanity? The debate is often focused upon the dark side of humanity, and whether or not Jesus was capable of sinning. Yet, making a mistake, such as dropping a bowl, is not presented as a result of sin in this segment. Instead, it is presented as simply part of being human. Jesus, the eternal Son of God, the creator of all things, is so thoroughly incarnated into humanity that he forever assumes all that it means to be positively human. Young presents Jesus's human condition as something that carries on into eternity.[18]

The submissive love of God is seen with clarity in the creation account in *Eve*. Here, creation as an expression of God's love takes precedence because God did not need to create anything or anyone. God has always been, and will always be, fully satisfied in his

14. Young, *Lies*, 201.
15. Young, *Lies*, 201.
16. Young, *Shack*, 104.
17. Young, *Shack*, 104.
18. Young, *Lies*, 226–27.

relationship with the other members of the Trinity. The choice to create is the desire to pour his triune love into creation simply for the purpose of loving. This purpose is seen in the extravagance of this creation, and how wastefully and abundantly this love is focused upon Earth. As Lilly, the main character observes, "communal Love was settled on one tiny, secluded, precisely constructed planet tucked inside the rim of a spiral galaxy."[19] This planet was created by the Spirit, whom Young describes as being "abandoned to the Father's love," through the "very being of Eternal Man."[20] The triune God, fully sufficient in its own love and being, paints into existence an extravagant universe with humanity at the very center of its worth. This love is not only expressed through creation, however. It is also expressed through God's nurturing of his creation. In language that is likely intentionally provoking of discussion, much in the same way the description of Papa as a "big black woman" was designed to subvert readers of their presuppositions about God,[21] Eternal Man is described as "nursing" Isha (Eve) at his breasts.[22] Here God's love is revealed in perhaps the most submissive imagery imaginable: the image of a mother vulnerably tending to the needs of her infant. Much in the same manner as with Papa in *The Shack*, this is not Young speaking in a literal fashion wherein he is asserting that Eternal Man had breasts. Rather, this is Young communicating the feminine side of God which, as revealed in *Eve*, he feels is quite neglected in our modern conceptions of God.[23]

This creative emphasis is also seen in *The Shack* where Mack and Jesus are sitting on the dock, looking at the stars. Jesus makes this poignant statement about his creative work in making the universe. He affirms that he created "as the Word" and that he now sits

19. Young, *Eve*, 170.
20. Young, *Eve*, 172.
21. Young, *Shack*, 86.
22. Young, *Eve*, 189.
23. See Brad Jersak, "Wm. Paul Young on Women," https://www.youtube.com/watch?v=iqZQLAvgIWc. In this conversation, Young talks about submission in the context of marriage and as it relates to women. His treatment of this is a critique of the Christian church's overall neglect of the value of women. In *Eve*, Young seems to be alluding to this.

The God Who Submits

as the Word made flesh enjoying his very own creation.[24] The God who created all is now enjoying his creation from a new perspective, a *human* perspective. No longer is Jesus only the Word, he is the Word made flesh. Such a description expresses the incarnate action of the Son, and expresses Young's understanding of God's power. To reiterate: Young does not believe in a deistic or passive God. To the contrary, Young believes in an extremely active God. However, God is not a tyrant, leading through supreme force. Instead, God is the Servant King of the universe who leads through power expressed in submissive love; a love which creates and then enters creation, facing existence from a different perspective. This new perspective is much more approachable for Mack who affirms that he is more comfortable around Jesus than Papa and Sarayu.[25] Mack says that Jesus is more "real" and "tangible" than Papa and Sarayu.[26] Here, Young is presenting what he views as one of the central aspects of the incarnation: the tangibility of God. Not only is God more approachable in Jesus, according to Young, but Jesus reveals the very nature of the Trinity in a meaningful and clear way to humanity.[27] This is a purely submissive action on Jesus's part. Jesus, in his essence as a human, has become human solely for the sake of humans. There is no other reason other than to love his creation from the most intimate perspective imaginable. Young presents Jesus's existence as a human not only with distinctly positive and normal human characteristics in mind. He also presents Jesus as being afflicted by the dark aspects of the human condition. Young affirms that at the crucifixion, Jesus *experienced* separation from the Father. Yet, Papa makes it clear that she was with Jesus on the cross through the revelation of scars on her own wrists.[28] She then states that Jesus merely *felt* abandoned, but that she had never actually left him.[29] Such an experience of abandonment is

---

24. Young, *Shack*, 109.
25. Young, *Shack*, 110.
26. Young, *Shack*, 110.
27. Young, *Shack*, 110.
28. Young, *Shack*, 96.
29. Young, *Shack*, 96.

A Love in the Key of Three: The Triune Community

symptomatic of the human condition. Young affirms that humanity often believes itself to be separated from God, or that God is somehow distanced from his creation. Yet, this is not the case. It is merely an experience or sensation of divine distance. This experience was encountered by Jesus on the cross. Jesus's submission to the human condition means submission to the Great Sadness in which all of humanity finds itself, a sadness built largely upon the myth of separation from God.

Another clear expression of God's submissive love is found in the Trinity's willingness to meet Mack at the shack where his daughter Missy was murdered, the core of Mack's Great Sadness.[30] A God who is not, in his nature, a servant, would seemingly make Mack come to his own personal throne for a meeting. Yet, such is not the case with the trinitarian God in Young's book. The Father, Son, and Spirit insert themselves into Mack's box and meet him in his own context. Perhaps it is for this reason that Papa's initial interaction with Mack is so powerful: Papa, depicted as a large black woman, lifts Mack off of his feet and passionately embraces him.[31] What is fascinating about this scene is Young's commentary on how Papa's actions had "breached every social propriety."[32] In other words, they had transcended relational borders and boundaries that had a certain preconceived etiquette all for the purpose of breathing love into the life of a severely tortured individual. God, it seems, is not concerned with relational or cultural walls. Instead, God is focused on transcending circumstance, and condescending into contexts, to love the individual. God, in Young's works, is not concerned about being polite. Gentle, perhaps, but not polite.

God's choice to submissively incarnate into Mack's broken world is also seen in the work of Papa, Jesus, and Sarayu in bringing closure to Mack's Great Sadness. These final steps are the last pieces of the puzzle for the foundation of his wholeness. Papa now manifests as a Native American man because, as he says, to

---

30. Young, *Shack*, 83.
31. Young, *Shack*, 83.
32. Young, *Shack*, 83.

The God Who Submits

accomplish these final steps Mack will need a father.[33] Here Young is not at all suggesting some form of modalism wherein God is one being who has different manifestations. Rather, this is Young's way of communicating the trans-circumstantial versatility of God's ability to incarnate into all circumstances for the individual. Yet why is father imagery used to express God in this final stage of Mack's journey? This is not a question to which Young provides a straightforward answer. Perhaps the choice to use masculine imagery in this section is best understood in light of his decision to present the feminine side of Papa during the previous chapters of the book. Before Papa changes, she is very much presented as a nurturer, always making food for Mack, and always providing a safe home to which Mack may always retreat. However, in this segment, Mack must journey into the very core of his own personal darkness, confronting the very root of his Great Sadness: Missy's murder. For this, Papa says, Mack will need a father to carry him in great strength and allow him to participate in this strength during this darkest time. Perhaps, then, Young is expressing this dichotomy of images to say something about both the inherent nurturing nature of God reflected in women, and the gentle—warrior nature of God reflected in men. Something similar to this is stated earlier in the book when Papa says that, because of the fall, genuine fathering is much more absent than mothering.[34] Perhaps this is Papa standing in the place of Mack's own father, being the type of father that Mack needed as a child. Perhaps Papa is being a father who rolls up his sleeves and gets dirty in the messiness of life with his children.

Mack must first forgive Missy's killer. This forgiveness is presented as being primarily for Mack's benefit to free him from his own lack of forgiveness, something that Papa says will destroy his "ability to love fully and openly" if not dealt with promptly.[35] Forgiveness is expressed as primarily about the individual harboring the resentment. Second, this forgiveness allows Mack to "release"

33. Young, *Shack*, 219.
34. Young, *Shack*, 94.
35. Young, *Shack*, 225.

A Love in the Key of Three: The Triune Community

the killer to Papa so that he can "redeem him."[36] Here, Young marries the concept of interpersonal forgiveness with God's redemption of the individual. Young seems to do this in order to express the idea that forgiveness is ultimately a change in perspective that desires the healing of the perpetrator. Papa desires to heal the Ladybug Killer for the same reason he desired to heal Mack: he too is Papa's son.[37] Young again presents an incarnational picture of God, but subtly with the Ladybug Killer in mind. Typically, in story, the villain is the individual we wish to see defeated. This is not so with Young's works. Young, in many ways, only tells stories about the redemption of villains as all are presented in the same light: hurting people in need of healing. After forgiving the killer, Mack needs to confront his darkness head on: he needs to find Missy's body and bury her. Mack sheds tears because of his gratitude to Papa for going on the journey to find Missy's body. Papa smiles at Mack and then "ever so gently" wipes his "tear-tracked cheeks."[38] Papa then says poignant words indicative of Young's view of God's ambition to heal his creation: "Mackenzie, this world is full of tears, but if you remember I promised that it would be Me who would wipe them from your eyes."[39] In this sentence, Young both presents the problem (humanity's need for healing) and God's incarnational action in the midst of this brokenness: he wipes the tears resulting from the human condition with his own hands, thereby carrying these tears on behalf of humanity.

God's desire to carry humanity's sorrows is also seen when Missy's body is found inside a cave. As Mack moves the rocks that hide the entrance, a pungent smell, presumably from Missy's body, hits Mack. Papa then pulls out a piece of linen and ties it around Mack's mouth.[40] This linen had been made by Sarayu for this very moment so that the smell of decay could be replaced with the smell

---

36. Young, *Shack*, 224.
37. Young, *Shack*, 224, 227.
38. Young, *Shack*, 228.
39. Young, *Shack*, 228.
40. Young, *Shack*, 229.

The God Who Submits

of Sarayu's gift.[41] Here again is the picture of a God who is in humanity's service: God does not remove the smell of the corpse, but instead, carries the burden with Mack. God, to heal the human condition, injects the sweet smell of love into the heart of the odorous, sin-afflicted existence of humanity.

Mack carries Missy's body back to Jesus's work shed. Jesus, after seeing Mack, "gently" relieves him of his "burden and together they went to the shop where he [Jesus] had been working."[42] Jesus then places Missy into a coffin that he had been making during the entirety of Mack's time with the Trinity.[43] The coffin is full of etchings in the wood depicting Missy's life and is so obviously an act of love and devotion from Jesus who took all the care in the world to provide a safe place for Mack's little girl.[44] This personal touch of Jesus's illustrates Young's understanding of how God's love is adapted to meet the circumstances of each of his children. This is not a one-size-fits-all love. Rather, this divine love is transcendent, penetrating each human life according to individual personalities and circumstances. God's submissive nature is also seen in Sarayu's collection of Mack's tears.[45] The tears are spread by Sarayu "onto the rich black soil under which Missy's body slept" causing flowers to bloom wherever the drops landed.[46] These tears, which were ultimately the result of tremendous human pain, are used by God for the redemption of the person. In *Cross Roads*, Young presents a similar context for God's healing: the tortured soul of Anthony Spencer, a man who was twisted by the loss of his son, Gabriel. In the work, the character known as Jack tells Anthony of God's ability to redeem even the vilest actions: "Somehow the pain, the losses, the hurt, the bad, God is able to transform these into something they could have never been, icons and monuments

41. Young, *Shack*, 229.
42. Young, *Shack*, 231.
43. Young, *Shack*, 231.
44. Young, *Shack*, 231.
45. Young, *Shack*, 84.
46. Young, *Shack*, 233.

of grace and love."⁴⁷ For Mack, Missy's death becomes a monument of grace and love through these actions of the Trinity which so vividly express the servant-heart of God and his desire to enter into humanity's darkened condition for the purpose of redeeming it.

COMPARING YOUNG AND THE INCARNATION THEOLOGY OF T.F. TORRANCE

Young's concept of God's submission finds parallel to T.F. Torrance's conception of Jesus's incarnation. Torrance's entire theology of incarnation seems to be founded upon the submissive love of the Son as he becomes the very darkness that he was sent to redeem. For Torrance, the nature of God is revealed and expressed fully in what he calls God's "condescension" into the life and existence of humanity through the incarnation.⁴⁸ The historical context for this condescension is the nation of Israel. Jesus was born as a Jew, becoming one with a nation that Torrance states had a "bitter and stubborn hatred of God's grace."⁴⁹ Torrance states further that Israel was "a beggarly and despised people, as Moses told them, and it proved itself to be the most stiff-necked and rebellious of peoples, but it was chosen out of pure love and on that basis alone was brought into covenant relation with God."⁵⁰ According to Torrance, Jesus incarnated into humanity through Israel, a nation who epitomizes the lostness of humanity. Jesus condescends into humanity's darkness and becomes submissive to this darkness,

---

47. Young, *Cross Roads*, 157.

48. Torrance, *Incarnation*, 43. See also St. Athanasius, *Incarnation*, 57. Athanasius's account of the incarnation uses similar language to Torrance: "Having mercy upon our race, and having pity upon our weakness, and condescending to our corruption, and not enduring the dominion of death, lest what had been created should perish and the work of the Father himself for human beings should be in vain, he takes for himself a body and that not foreign to our own."

49. Torrance, *Incarnation*, 42.

50. Torrance, *Incarnation*, 46.

The God Who Submits

through his incarnation as a Jew. For Torrance, this was God's way of identifying with humanity on a grand scale.[51]

The incarnation into human existence through Israel is not merely an abstract philosophical metaphor or intellectual concept for Torrance. Rather, it is the point in time when the Son of God assumed "human nature into oneness with himself."[52] The Son of God, who made all things, becomes a man and assumes the "bondage and estrangement of humanity fallen from God and under the divine judgement."[53] This flesh assumed by Jesus is indeed the very flesh "marked by Adam's fall," according to Torrance.[54] This assumption of human flesh is a critical foundation for Torrance's theology for, as he quotes St. Gregory of Nazianzus, "the unassumed is the unredeemed."[55] If Jesus did not assume the total and utter fallenness of our human nature, if his condescension means something other than this, then humanity is not redeemed. To quote further from St. Gregory, Jesus "was actually subject as a slave to flesh, to birth, and to our human experiences; for our liberation, held captive as we are by sin, he was subject to all that he saved;"[56] and "as the 'form of a slave' he comes down to the same level as his fellow-slaves; receiving an alien 'form' he bears the whole of me, along with all that is mine, in himself, so that he may consume within himself the meaner element, as fire consumes wax or the Sun ground mist, and so that I may share in what is his through the intermingling."[57] For both Torrance and St. Gregory, an incarnation divorced from the actual condition of humanity is an incarnation void of meaning. If the incarnation is somehow independent of fallen human flesh, then Jesus cannot address humankind from within its context. Rather, he speaks to humanity on the outside

---

51. Torrance, *Incarnation*, 57.
52. Torrance, *Incarnation*, 57.
53. Torrance, *Incarnation*, 61.
54. Torrance, *Incarnation*, 61.
55. Torrance, *Incarnation*, 62.
56. St. Gregory, *God and Christ*, 94–95.
57. St. Gregory, *God and Christ*, 97.

A Love in the Key of Three: The Triune Community

of its existence in a disconnected manner.[58] For Torrance, Jesus's own person and being becomes a "word" or message to humanity precisely because he meets humanity as a human, translating or communicating the heart of God to a rebellious creation.[59] It is from within humanity that the Son "exegetes" the Father and "reveals him to and within human life on earth and in history."[60] The Father, Son, and Holy Spirit had a mission to translate themselves for humanity through the Son.

There exists a clear parallel between Torrance's understanding of the incarnation or condescension of Jesus and the submissive God in Young's theology. For Young, as much as submissive love has always existed within the Trinity, the human condition has obscured the possibility of understanding this nature of God. There exists a need for a penetration of the human condition, a communication of the nature of God in a language understood by humanity. This seems to be the purpose of the incarnation as Young understands it. As seen when Jesus is sitting with Mack on the dock, there exists a familiarity in Jesus as he reveals or expresses the nature of Papa and Sarayu to Mack. This, in microcosm, is how Young views the incarnation. Without the incarnation, there is no true understanding of God. Young is not concerned about presenting a systematic or dogmatic theology, as is Torrance. Young presents written experiences of God which subtly communicate divine truths. When Papa speaks to the idea of her abandonment of Jesus on the cross, she is alluding to the experience Jesus had because he was human. This is not a mechanical or robotic Jesus who did not experience all that it means to be human: Jesus became the very essence of the human condition both in benign aspects (i.e. Jesus drops a bowl) and in those aspects which are the direct result of the sin affliction (i.e. "my God my God why have you forsaken me?"). In both Torrance and Young, Jesus is real in the purest, most human way. He is approachable and he is relatable. The incarnation is essentially and actually the most intimate expression

---

58. Torrance, *Incarnation*, 68.
59. Torrance, *Incarnation*, 68.
60. Torrance, *Incarnation*, 68.

The God Who Submits

of God's submissive love. For Torrance, St. Gregory, and Young, God's unrelenting love expresses itself through saying "Yes" to that human condition in which we find ourselves.

ENCOUNTERING YOUNG

When Young argues that God is submissive by nature, he is not negating the sovereignty or power of God. He is arguing that God exerts his power in a different way than human-made gods: God exerts his power through the withholding of his power. He does not use his power to coerce, though he could and has at times in salvation history (I'm thinking of Paul's encounter with Jesus on the Damascus road, for example). Yet, this is the exception and not the rule. In fact, encounters such as the one with Paul do not negate the importance God places on the response of the individual. While we read Scripture, it may appear that some individuals never really had a choice to follow God, or to behave in the way they did (Pharaoh as an example).[61] But a submissive nature always leaves room for decision, and always honors the decision of the individual. This is the plight of God's triune love, according to Young. What Young does so helpfully is find ways to express the servant heart of God in a manner that demands all other attributes of God be understood in light of it. God's love, justice, wrath, atonement, and any other attribute or action of his, must be understood in light of his love expressed through submission. Young forces his readers to confront their understanding of God's love and to build all beliefs upon this love. His views of submission

---

61. The account of Pharaoh is interesting because God's hardening of Pharaoh's heart, and Pharaoh's own hardening, are spoken of synonymously and interchangeably in the text. Furthermore, the phrase in Exod 9:12, "But the Lord hardened Pharaoh's heart" (NASB), is somewhat obscure. It is unclear from the passage whether this is a direct supernatural hardening from God, or whether Pharaoh was simply angry at Yahweh of his own volition. If one takes a more Calvinistic approach to the text, then the hardening would likely be supernatural in origin. However, the latter view may be preferred if operating in a different framework. If this latter view is true, then Pharaoh had a volitional decision to make independent of divine action.

A Love in the Key of Three: The Triune Community

bring action to the love of God which without such a concept is mere high theological reasoning. Submission is love in action, and Young's exploration of this subject in the context of specific human circumstances demonstrates the tangibility of God's love in the heart of life's circumstances.

Young is very much operating within the themes of two passages from Scripture: Phil 2:7 and the relationship between Christ and the church depicted in Eph 5:22–33. Phil 2:5–7 reads as follows: "Have this attitude in yourselves which was also in Christ Jesus, who, as He already existed in the form of God, did not consider equality with God something to be grasped, but emptied Himself by taking the form of a bond-servant and being born in the likeness of men" (NASB). The context of the passage is Christian behavior: Christians are to imitate Christ's humility in their interactions with one another. The reason why this is such a powerful statement is that Christ, who was and is God, did not use his Godhood as a means of exerting power. Instead, he "emptied Himself" by serving and becoming human. He limited himself for love. The implications of this are far-reaching as we see explored in Young. Christ certainly emptied himself in a historical context. However, let's not forget that he revealed the nature of God (Col 1 and Heb 1). As Young rightly affirms, this revelation not only shows that Jesus is a servant, but that the entirety of the Godhead is inherently submissive to the needs of humanity and seeks to love humanity through servitude. God, through the Holy Spirit, transcends our every circumstance to offer himself to us.

Eph 5:22–33 paints a very similar picture to Phil 2:5–7. While many see this passage primarily as a depiction of how Christian marriages are to work, I argue that that this passage is more about Christ's relationship with the church than human marriage, as present as this topic is in the section. Paul is very clear: Christ is a servant who offered himself for the church in order that he might save it (Eph 5:25–26). Paul also describes Christ's ongoing ministry with the church to nourish and cherish it (Eph 5:29). Christ continues to tend to the church, taking care to love and serve it and maintain it. In the context, this is what Paul means by stating that

The God Who Submits

Christ is the head of the church (Eph 5:22). Christ is the authority over the church but he uses his authority to nourish and serve the church. This does not at all mean that the church owns Jesus in some way. To the contrary, it means that there is inherent power to sacrificial love and God relates to us in this power. He is not seeking to steamroll us with his power. Instead, he washes our feet in order to love for that is who he is at the core of his being. Young seems to apply this to his concept of the submissive love of God. God condescends into our lives in order to reveal himself to us. I can think of no more poignant Christian conviction.

CHAPTER 3

THE GOD WITHOUT A RELIGION

AS WE'VE SEEN, THE LOVE of the Father, Son, and Spirit is not a passive love for Young. To the contrary, it is a love of action from which God seeks to reach his creation in any and every possible context. This understanding of God's love as action, or verb, is the foundation for Young's assertion that God exists apart from religion and therefore transcends all religions.

The concept of knowing God, apart from religion, is one that has gained noticeable traction over the last sixty years or so. It is a theme seemingly reflected in the Jesus Movement of the sixties and seventies in which so-called "flower children" found Christianity and began a movement focused on free expression of faith independent of organized Christian institutions (an action likely reflective of their general rejection of human systems). Usually when the phrase is used in modern times, it speaks of the desire for a pure relationship with Jesus apart from any human-made system. Works such as Andrew Farley's *God Without Religion* apply this concept to salvation, arguing that Jesus's work was completely sufficient for our salvation, and that believers are to know and enjoy Jesus instead of living lives of legalistic religious obligation

The God Without a Religion

to God.¹ Such authors as Brennan Manning, who expressed the importance of relationship with God apart from rules and regulations, and also Max Lucado across his vast body of writings, seek to express the importance of letting God guide the individual into a relationship with himself based upon freedom from rules and regulations.

Young operates in much the same way though some of his theology is certainly different than these authors. He expresses the dire consequences of mixing human-made religion with relationship with God. He also applies the concept as it relates to the transcendence of God amongst the religions of the world. While Young does not believe that God is affiliated with human-made institutions be they religious or secular, he is convinced that God does incarnate into these institutions in order to win people over to relationship with himself. This includes the institution of Christianity. Some have taken Young's views to communicate a form of religious pluralism.² Thus, it is beneficial to explore Young's understanding of knowing God apart from religion within the context of religious pluralism that the sheer differences between the two frameworks may be understood.

One of the primary passages in Young's works said to teach religious pluralism is found in *The Shack*.³ Jesus affirms that he is personally not a Christian, and that people who know him come from all different types of human-made institutions, Christian, non-Christian, and secular (such as political parties).⁴ Mack finds this revelation shocking and inquires as to whether or not this means that "all roads" lead to God.⁵ Jesus rejects such a concept: "Most roads don't lead anywhere. What it does mean, is that I will

---

1. Farley, *God Without Religion*, 10.
2. See Perkins, "Why 'The Shack' is Blasphemous," https://compass.org/article-why-the-shack-is-blasphemous/.
3. Perkins, "Why 'The Shack' is Blasphemous," https://compass.org/article-why-the-shack-is-blasphemous/.
4. Young, *Shack*, 182.
5. Young, *Shack*, 182.

A Love in the Key of Three: The Triune Community

travel down any road to find you."[6] While the passage could potentially be read to denote pluralism, close inspection reveals the precise opposite of pluralism. Young presents God as an immersive missionary. God is expressed as transcending human conceptions of himself, and subverting ideas about who he is within various missionary contexts (Mack's broken soul or his own Christian religion, for example). Yet, God does this while maintaining his rightful place as the Lord of all without compromising his identity. At no point in *The Shack* does God acknowledge salvation as being part of any other path but the one which leads to Jesus (or rather the path which is Jesus himself). Young is quite clear: there is no salvation apart from Christ, and there is no God but the Trinity of Scripture. Young's views about God's relationship to human-made religion are within the context of presenting God as incarnationally working within all human religions and systems to reach his creation. Young's point in *The Shack* is not that people are saved through adherence to the Buddhist faith or Muslim faith, for example, but rather that people are not saved through adherence to any religion. People are saved through relationship with the Jesus who travels down all of humanity's roads, entering into each of its contexts, in order to invite all to relationship with the triune God of love.

Similar language is found in *Cross Roads* though with some emphases that provoke thought in a different manner. When Tony is talking to Jesus about the nature of the Trinity he asks if Christians are polytheists because they believe in three gods.[7] Jesus states that this is not what is meant at all and affirms that there is one God, but he exists in three persons.[8] However, Jesus affirms that there are many non-Christian people who believe in him without fully comprehending his identity.[9] Jesus then lists Muslims, Jews, and Greek philosophers as included among

---

6. Young, *Shack*, 182.
7. Young, *Cross Roads*, 71.
8. Young, *Cross Roads*, 71.
9. Young, *Cross Roads*, 71.

The God Without a Religion

these people.[10] Young seems to be arguing that the existence of other monotheistic faiths is proof of God's activity among them. Yet, as with *The Shack*, at no point does Young argue for a form of religious pluralism. Rather, Young is expressing the commonality between different monotheistic religions and suggesting that individuals within these faiths may have some interaction with the triune God, even if they do not know it. Young is stirring the conversational waters here. In Young's view, no religion, whether Christian or non-Christian, saves. God saves through relationship with the Son, a relationship that ushers the individual into intimacy with the Father, Son, and Spirit. As Young states in *Lies We Believe about God*, not only is God not a Christian, he is not a member of any religion.[11] Consequently, God does not treat non-Christians, or anyone, as outsiders because they do not operate within the Christian faith.[12] To the contrary, Young views all people as existing inside of God's unending, ever enveloping, trinitarian love.[13] Because all exist within the love of God, God can and does seek to impact people within their contexts for all contexts exist within his love and presence.[14] Knowing God apart from religion means recognizing that God wants a relationship with every human being apart from rules and regulations. In order to have this relationship, God submits to our religious systems in order to meet us in the midst of these boundaries.[15] Precisely how this is the case, is not clear. How might this work out in a real-world context in, say, the faith of a Muslim or a Buddhist? Maybe some answers will present themselves as we compare Young and Lewis.

10. Young, *Cross Roads*, 72–73.
11. Young, *Lies*, 54.
12. Young, *Lies*, 55.
13. Young, *Lies*, 55.
14. Young, *Lies*, 55.
15. Young, *Lies*, 109.

A Love in the Key of Three: The Triune Community

YOUNG AND C.S. LEWIS'S *THE LAST BATTLE*

Perhaps Young has in mind themes similar to those expressed at the conclusion of C.S. Lewis's *The Last Battle*. In Lewis's work, Emeth is a Calormene officer who has served Tash, the false God in the work, since he was a little boy.[16] He served Tash so fervently that even "the name of Aslan was hateful" to him.[17] When Emeth met Aslan in Aslan's Country, he expected condemnation for worshipping a false god. Yet, Aslan does not condemn Emeth. Instead, he welcomes him to the Country. Emeth asks, "Lord, is it true, as the Ape said, that thou and Tash are one?"[18] After letting out a large growl, Aslan responds with these poignant words:

> It is false. Not because he and I are one, but because we are opposites–I take to me the services which thou hast done to him. Therefore, if any man sweat by Tash and keep his oath for the oath's sake, it is by me that he has truly sworn, though he know it not, and it is I who reward him. And if any man do a cruelty in my name, then, though he says the name Aslan, it is Tash whom he serves and by Tash his deed is accepted.[19]

Furthermore, Aslan, before disappearing, tells Emeth that "unless thy desire had been for me thou wouldst not have sought so long and so truly. For all find what they truly seek."[20] Lewis seems to be commenting on God's accommodation of the earnest desire existent within humans to know him, even if they are seeking him through their own religious context (similar to Young's language about monotheistic religions in *Cross Roads*). Lewis also seems to suggest that God sees these intentions and, in a manner of speaking, reveals himself as the answer to these deep desires whenever he is seen clearly by the individual. Here, Lewis, like Young, does not appear to affirm multiple paths to God. To the

16. Lewis, *Last Battle*, 755.
17. Lewis, *Last Battle*, 755
18. Lewis, *Last Battle*, 757.
19. Lewis, *Last Battle*, 757.
20. Lewis, *Last Battle*, 757.

The God Without a Religion

contrary, Lewis presents Aslan as the one, true, God against whom all false gods are judged. However, there is an element of divine transcendence and accommodation expressed in Aslan's language that perhaps has some parallel to Young.

Religion, for Young, is the result of humanity's desire to know God though, to be sure, it is a far cry from *knowing* God. Nevertheless, it is an earnest attempt to know him not dissimilar from Emeth's journey in Lewis's story. Young is certainly not interested in making absolute statements about how God works in every context: the nature of relationship with God suggests a potential myriad of ways that he can reach people. However, Young does seem to suggest, along with Lewis, that human religion does not exclude the possibility that God will transcend earthly religious contexts in unique ways while retaining his true identity. Thus, it could be that Young's views find a potential practical expression in Lewis's account of Emeth. Perhaps Young would say that God judges the intention of the individual, and that earnest individuals in all faiths will see, in Jesus, the reality of all they had hoped for in life.[21]

COMPARING YOUNG AND JOHN HICK'S RELIGIOUS PLURALISM

John Hick, a religious pluralist, operates in a noticeably different framework than Lewis and Young. Whereas Young's entire relational theology depends upon the literal incarnation of the Son, Hick rejects a literal incarnation, and consequently, does not view Christianity as the ultimate source of truth.[22] Hick maintains that if Jesus was God incarnate, then Christianity would certainly be the only pure religion. However, Hick finds such a claim problematic and insensitive to the claims of other faiths.[23] Hick's understanding

---

21. This concept could lead to universalism if the assumption is made that all people will believe once they see Jesus clearly. Yet, such a conclusion seems odd given the rejection of Christ during his earthly ministry.

22. Hick, *God Has Many Names*, 8 and 19 and *Theology of Religions*, 91.

23. Hick, *Theology of Religions*, 87.

of religious pluralism exists atop this rejection of a literal incarnation, as well as the existence of other faiths.

For Hick, religious pluralism is the recognition of two central tenets. First, that there does exist an ultimate God, a God whom Hick refers to as the "Eternal One."[24] For Hick, this God is not clearly known or understood though, interestingly, Hick also refers to "Reality" (another name for the "Eternal One") as transcendent.[25] However, whereas Young views the incarnation as the expression of divine transcendence, Hick sees the existence of other faiths as the proof of divine transcendence.[26] This ambiguously defined God seems to allow Hick freedom to keep from presenting God as being contained or expressed fully by any one religion. Here Hick finds parallel with his own understanding of Hinduism which he presents as based upon the premise that the "Reality" is beyond human categories and can thus not be defined.[27]

The second tenet is the existence of a sheer number of different faiths in the world, and the friendships Hick holds with different members of these faiths.[28] Hick maintains that these devoted members of different religions are all "savingly related to the eternal Reality from which we all live."[29] It is this "accumulated knowledge of the other great faiths" that leads Hick to conclude that a shared expression of the Eternal One exists within each of the major world religions.

Hick's criteria for discerning this shared expression is twofold. First, Hick maintains that longevity of a belief system is characteristic of it being a reflection of the Eternal One:

> When we are confronted by a stream of religious life and thought and experience that has persisted for many centuries, which has produced inspiring scriptures and a rich succession of saints and prophets and profound

24. Hick, *God Has Many Names*, 22.
25. Hick, *God Has Many Names*, 22.
26. Hick, *God Has Many Names*, 42.
27. Hick, *God Has Many Names*, 120.
28. Hick, *God Has Many Names*, 17.
29. Hick, *God Has Many Names*, 18.

The God Without a Religion

thinkers, and has provided a spiritual home in which hundreds of millions of human lives have been lived, then I think we have to assume that it represents a genuine awareness of and response to the Eternal One.[30]

Hick, when affirming religious pluralism, is not speaking of tribal religions which have not survived the test of time. Rather, in addition to Christianity, he is speaking of religions like "Hinduism, Judaism, Buddhism, Jainism, Taoism, Confucianism, Islam, Sikhism, and Baha'i."[31] Second according to Hick, the main world religions express what Christianity calls the "fruits of the spirit" within their own contexts.[32] Hick argues that these "visible fruits do not occur more abundantly among Christians than among Jews, Muslims, Hindus, Buddhists, Sikhs, Taoists, Baha'is, and so on. And yet surely they ought to if the situation were as it is pictured in our traditional Christian theology."[33] Hick, therefore, seems to view moral output as a significant indicator for what is genuinely a reflection of the Eternal One. Yet, problematically, Hick's theological net is so wide that it does not account for the diversity of moral actions possible. For example, Hick seems to focus primarily on how humans are to treat one another in terms of kindness and love (i.e. the "golden rule" or treating others the way one wants to be treated).[34] However, he does not recognize the inconsistency which arises out of cherry-picking certain moral ideals seemingly reflective of the Eternal One while rejecting others that are supposedly not reflective of God such as the exclusivity claims regarding salvation in Christianity and Islam. What arises from Hick's thinking is a genuinely subjective recognition of what is reflective of God and what is not. Such a subjective view is no doubt allowed because of his rejection of the incarnation of Jesus. This rejection allows for Hick to determine his own view of truth. The desire of Hick to include the faiths of the world under one banner seems to

30. Hick, *God Has Many Names*, 56.
31. Hick, *Theology of Religions*, 12.
32. Hick, *Theology of Religions*, 14, 16.
33. Hick, *Theology of Religions*, 16.
34. Hick, *God Has Many Names*, 24.

A Love in the Key of Three: The Triune Community

arise out of genuine compassion for people. However, Hick's rejection of the incarnation creates this overly subjective moralistic filter used to determine each religions connection to the Eternal One. Young, in embracing the incarnation, seems to offer a better, more biblically grounded, response to the religions of the world. For Young, while all are inside of the love of the triune God, God has made himself ultimately and clearly known in Jesus. While Young believes God is outside of human-made religion, he does believe that Jesus entered into the human system, full of its religions, sects, and relational boundaries, in order to reveal the true God. Young also believes that this missionary effort of God continues today. Yet, Young is careful to not place stringent boundaries on how God can reach people. It is conceivable that God could find ways to transcend the religion of Islam, for example, in order to reveal himself in the person of Jesus in some manner. Yet if this were to occur, it would not be in some form other than Jesus.

ENCOUNTERING YOUNG

Young's approach to other religions offers an alternative to pluralism as expressed in Hick. In fact, it is critical to not even label Young as a "pluralist" even if to simply avoid over-association with the concept. Young certainly believes in and affirms the universal action of God for humanity. He insists on the ongoing incarnation of Christ into our lives and human experiences. Such concepts arise out of a clear compassion that Young holds for humanity. What makes Young's views standout is the compatibility they have with the necessary particularism of Jesus Christ: Young does not neglect Jesus as the only way to God. Yet, he blends this conviction with a missional love for people that he sees emanating from the heart of God. For those who have deep compassion for the world, and wish the very best for all, a mindset can be adopted that does not negate the importance of Jesus's incarnation and its implications for the revelation of the one true God. What Young does, quite helpfully, is present the transcendence of God as a direct expression of his trinitarian love while honoring the true

The God Without a Religion

identity of God and expressing a just compassion for people from all backgrounds.

Young's views have a strong compatibility with the depiction of the Holy Spirit in John 16:8: "And when he comes, he will convict the world concerning sin and righteousness and judgment" (ESV). Young applies this scriptural truth in a very tangible manner. If God is convicting the *world* of sin, righteousness and judgment, then he is necessarily doing this within the context of the world system. Young's convictions about God's transcendence seem to offer an application of John 16:8 that potentially resolves questions concerning the eternal destiny of those who have never heard the gospel. Such a concern is quite human-centric indeed. If we are not careful, we will think that God only goes into the parts of the world that we do. However, God does not need us to participate with him though he certainly wants us to do so. Thus, because God does not need us, it stands to reason that he is already at work in the world whether we are there or not.

CHAPTER 4

THE GOD WHO IS LIGHT

THE PHRASE "GOD IS GOOD," while simple on the surface, is not as easily understood as one might expect. To know if God is good, for example, a few presuppositions must be grasped. First, who is God, and second, what exactly is goodness? If God is a singular person without community within himself, then good is the result of a single testimony to the definition of the word (much like the case with love). Hence, whatever this God says is good, is good. However, if God is triune, as is the case with the biblical God, then goodness comes out of a community of persons each in infinite agreement on the meaning of the word while also offering a threefold testimony affirming the definition of good. All subjectivity, therefore, is non-existent in this triune community and in place of subjectivity is absolute truth confirmed by, and arising from, three witnesses. Goodness, by definition, if it arises out of God, must carry God's own spiritual DNA. To say that goodness is independent of God, or even that aspects of goodness are independent of God, is to present a goodness that is somehow existent apart from God's character. This brings us to the second presupposition.

The second presupposition, the nature of goodness, can only be understood if the nature of God is comprehended. If God is love at the core of his essence, for example, then goodness must

The God Who is Light

arise from love. Furthermore, in order for goodness to be defined, love must be definable and knowable. Goodness, therefore, cannot contradict love in any manner otherwise it completely ceases to be goodness. Consequently, goodness must be knowable alongside of love: there cannot exist any hidden corners to God's love or goodness that contradict what we know to be true of it. God cannot, for example, always express the fruits of the Spirit (Galatians 5:22–23) while simultaneously being an overly critical, impatient deity. In order for this to occur there would have to be some hidden aspect to love and goodness that is not obvious to humanity. Yet, as C.S. Lewis states so clearly, to say this is to say that "God is we know not what."[1] Lewis goes on to say that if "our idea of good is worth simply nothing" then worshipping this God is akin to worshipping the devil![2] Lewis concludes that our idea of goodness cannot differ from God's idea of goodness as "white" differs from "black."[3] Rather, our idea of goodness differs as a "perfect circle from a child's first attempt to draw a wheel."[4] The concept, the *knowing* of what is good is present. However, the understanding of the *depth* of goodness is rudimentary. For Lewis, the goodness of God is goodness as humanity understands it, in fullest expression and clarity. Consequently, humanity can know the goodness of God and know that his goodness does not contain any hidden attributes that will contradict other aspects of goodness. Young operates within this framework.

For Young, God's goodness is absolutely knowable because his character has been fully revealed in Christ. This goodness does not contain any hidden attributes that are contradictory to what is known plainly about this love that Jesus has so fully revealed. As Young claims, "God is light and in him is no darkness at all."[5] Young's point here is that if God is somehow the author of evil then

---

1. Lewis, *Problem of Pain*, 28.
2. Lewis, *Problem of Pain*, 29.
3. Lewis, *Problem of Pain*, 30.
4. Lewis, *Problem of Pain*, 30.
5. Young, FGC 2016 Session 11, 43 minutes. See also Young, *Lies*, 145. He is quoting from 1 John 1:5.

A Love in the Key of Three: The Triune Community

there exists some hidden aspect to God's goodness that is contradictory to our own understanding of goodness. However, Young articulates clearly that this cannot be the case: if God is the author of evil, in any way, then Young claims, in similarity to Lewis, that he cannot be trusted.[6] Therefore, God's goodness is knowable to humanity and, at least foundationally, looks like humanity's conception of goodness. For Young, divine goodness is always associated with divine love. Anything that is compatible with God's love is reflective of his goodness. Evil exists, therefore, not because God authors it but rather because he respects our decision to say "no" to him and live our lives independently of relationship with him (he submits to our decisions).[7] Evil originates with human decisions. However, God does not abandon humanity to its evil. Young believes that God's love compels him to not rest until all that is not of "love's kind" is gone from his creation.[8] For Young, God has one mission: love his creation. This love is not a passive love, but a love that seeks to purify creation from all darkness, a darkness caused by humans, and not God.

Young's understanding of God's goodness is seen in his analysis of the cross. According to Young, the cross is not good in any way.[9] To the contrary it is a device designed to inflict profound pain by keeping the crucified alive as long as possible.[10] If God originated the cross, says Young, then "we worship a cosmic child abuser."[11] The cross is not reflective of a God of light, according to

---

6. Young, FGC 2016 Session 11, https://www.youtube.com/watch?v=vcHX1p2AJ6U.

7. Young, FGC 2016 Session 11, https://www.youtube.com/watch?v=vcHX1p2AJ6U. See also Young, *Shack*, 190.

8. Young, FGC 2016 Session 11, https://www.youtube.com/watch?v=vcHX1p2AJ6U. See MacDonald, *Unspoken Sermons*, 17–23. Young has unmistakable parallels to the writings of George MacDonald. MacDonald states that divine love "loves unto purity" for the individual (17). For MacDonald, the consuming fire of divine judgement is love seeking the healing of the individual.

9. Young, *Lies*, 149.

10. Young, *Lies*, 149.

11. Young, *Lies*, 149.

The God Who is Light

Young. Rather, it is reflective of the darkness within human beings.[12] The cross is the "ultimate fist raised against God" by humanity as it destroys that which God has created.[13] Death, therefore, has no place in God because life is the essence of God's being. However, Young believes that God's goodness was manifested at the cross. God willingly submitted to the cross and to humanity's desire to murder to destroy the power of the cross as a torture device, and consequently, the power of violent darkness on the earth.[14] For Young the love of God is revealed in his honoring of humanity's decision to murder him (the ultimate application of submission as discussed in chapter 2), and in his redemption of humanity in the midst of this murder. Young also seems to have in mind the resurrection of Jesus though it is not stated overtly in this section.[15] The resurrection is the pure expression of God's life being infused once again into the incarnate Lord thereby demonstrating the inverse of the cross. Young also affirms that God's forgiveness of the world occurred at the cross. This is alluded to in *The Shack* when Papa states that he has forgiven humanity in Christ.[16] This is not to say that Christ was a mechanism for this forgiveness, but rather, that God forgave in midst of the crucifixion.[17] Young seems to have in mind the meaning of *hilastērion* (Greek for "propitiation") which denotes not an appeasement of God's wrath, but rather, the Mercy Seat or location of forgiveness. God's goodness, therefore, was revealed in his forgiveness of humanity in the midst of the crucifixion of Jesus. God took the very horrendous act of Jesus's crucifixion and made it into redemption for those who crucified him.

Young's understanding of divine goodness is also seen in *Eve* when Eternal Man, after holding Adam close to his chest during the creation account, looks at the main character, Lilly, who is witnessing this event. When Eternal Man looks at her, Lilly feels "His

12. Young, *Lies*, 149.
13. Young, *Lies*, 149.
14. Young, *Lies*, 150.
15. Young, *Lies*, 150
16. Young, *Shack*, 225.
17. Young mentions this in a personal email sent to me on March 19, 2019.

A Love in the Key of Three: The Triune Community

peace wash through and over her."[18] This peace relieves her of the burden she is carrying.[19] The creation account in *Eve* is one of the most beautiful artistic expressions of creation written. One of the primary reasons for this, and why it deserves thought, is that we see God's goodness tangibly expressed before sin enters the world. The fact that God was good from eternity past necessitates that God is still good today for goodness is his nature independent of humanity's existence. This goodness is seen later when God and Adam sit down together in God's creation. God, here described as Adonai, turns and looks at Lilly, smiling and nodding in greeting.[20] This greeting causes Lilly to feel pure acceptance from God.[21] Lilly then sees Adonai tell Adam that he is "the center of Our affection and the radiance of Our glory."[22] Young's portrayal of creation so clearly expresses a goodness that has always been, yet is now, being given to humanity. Humanity is not the first to partake of this goodness, for the Trinity has always been good, but humanity is finding itself situated in the center of goodness.

A brief, though critical, conversation about the goodness of God takes place between Mack and Papa in *The Shack*. Mack and Papa are talking about Papa's interactions with his children and whether or not he ever has anger towards them. Papa admits that he does have anger, but that anger is simply another expression of love.[23] But this anger is ultimately revealed as a response to the sin that damages his creation and is associated with God's desire to heal his creation of sin.[24] This conception of anger is paralleled with Mack's misunderstandings about God's killing of people in the Old Testament, and also the nature of hell.[25] For Young, hell seems to largely be the experience of sinful choices, not the anger

18. Young, *Eve*, 41.
19. Young, *Eve*, 41
20. Young, *Eve*, 62.
21. Young, *Eve*, 62.
22. Young, *Eve*, 62.
23. Young, *Shack*, 119.
24. Young, *Shack*, 120.
25. Young, *Shack*, 119.

The God Who is Light

of God.[26] Interestingly, Young does not directly address the violent imagery of the Old Testament God in this passage. Furthermore, Young has not addressed the topic in great detail though he has addressed it some with the story of Abram. Young articulates that if we were to rate Abram on the scale of spiritual maturity, from A–Z, Abram would be somewhere between A and B (immature).[27] Young argues that this immaturity is the exact reason why Abram held appeasement theology and was so willing to sacrifice his son to God and why his son was so willing to be sacrificed.[28] God, in an effort to insert himself into Abram's context, then provides a sacrifice for Abram. This, Young believes, occurs because God is stating, in no uncertain terms, that he is not like the typical Ancient Near Eastern gods who demanded sacrifice, and instead, is good to the core of his being not demanding sacrificial practices.[29] Furthermore, Young affirms, citing the prophets, that God hates sacrifice thereby further presenting God as both transcendent into Abram's context yet wholly different from pagan deities.[30] Young seems to indicate that before Christ, people had an incomplete understanding of God's goodness, yet, God chose to interfere in various aspects of pre–Christ history in order give a glimpse of himself within their context.[31]

---

26. Young, *Shack*, 120.

27. Young, FGC Session 11, https://www.youtube.com/watch?v=vcHX1p2AJ6U.

28. Young, FGC Session 11, https://www.youtube.com/watch?v=vcHX1p2AJ6U.

29. Young, FGC Session 11, https://www.youtube.com/watch?v=vcHX1p2AJ6U.

30. Young, FGC Session 11, https://www.youtube.com/watch?v=vcHX1p2AJ6U.

31. Though Young does not say this overtly, it seems clear from his message that God was not known well by Israel pre-Christ. Given what Young believes about divine love and divine life, it seems that all violence is inherently not of God. This would also include the conquest narratives of the Old Testament and other violent passages ascribed to God. For more on Young's view of violence and how it is contradictory to the goodness of God see Young, "The Killing House," http://wmpaulyoung.com/the-killing-house/.

Another critical conversation in *The Shack* is when Mack challenges the goodness of God by questioning how the murder of his little girl could be part of a good God's plan.[32] Papa affirms that God is not evil, but that evil is the result of humanity choosing a life of independence from God. Missy's murder is presented as a result of this. Yet, Papa affirms that God will take every choice humanity makes and use it for good and "the most loving outcome."[33] Furthermore, Papa affirms that there are many reasons to allow tragedy and suffering into people's lives but that those reasons are only understood within the context of "each person's story."[34] Young creates a solid dichotomy between the goodness of God and human suffering, whether it is caused by sin or tragedy. To be sure, nothing that is contrary to life is of God, according to Young. However, God's goodness is revealed in his allowance of human free will and also the ultimate outcome of human history wherein God brings all things under the captivity of his goodness and love.[35] The key is whether or not one trusts that God is good in the midst of the chaos of life. Papa says as much to Mack when he confronts Mack's unbelief in his goodness.[36]

COMPARING YOUNG AND CALVINIST CONCEPTIONS OF GOD'S GOODNESS

Young's view of God's goodness is in stark contrast to the typical presentation of God's sovereignty articulated by John Calvin and those who share clear parallels to his thinking. Calvin states that while God "contracts no taint" from the impurity of evil actions,[37] and is "exempt from all guilt,"[38] he still directs the malice of evil

---

32. Young, *Shack*, 125.
33. Young, *Shack*, 125.
34. Young, *Shack*, 125.
35. Young, *Shack*, 126.
36. Young, *Shack*, 126.
37. Calvin, *Institutes*, 135.
38. Calvin, *Institutes*, 135.

The God Who is Light

persons "to whatever end he pleases."[39] Calvin states that humans are "blinded by the will and command of God" to do evil and are then condemned and punished for this blindness by God himself.[40] Humankind can "do nothing save at the secret instigation of God" and cannot "discuss and deliberate on any thing but what has previously been decreed" by God.[41] Calvin's view of God's goodness is decidedly antithetical to Lewis's view stated at the beginning of the chapter, and would likely lead Lewis to conclude that "God is we know not what." Young would have a difficult time trusting such a God for if God does act in such a way, authoring evil through his vessels and then condemning these vessels for their actions, then he cannot be trusted because his idea of goodness is wholly different from ours.

Calvin's sentiments are also echoed by Desiring God writer Joe Rigney when he states that everything, good and bad is, "ordained, guided, and governed by the creator and sustainer of the universe."[42] Similarly, Wayne Grudem, in his massive Systematic Theology work, affirms that God does "cause evil events to come about and evil deeds to be done."[43] Yet, Grudem also affirms that "Scripture nowhere shows God as directly doing anything evil, but rather bringing about evil deeds through the willing actions of moral creatures."[44] Perhaps Grudem's language best articulates the potentially confusing semantics that occur when simultaneously maintaining the goodness of God alongside of the statement that God is behind every event, good and evil. Grudem's language seems to take Calvin's more ardent emphasis on God being the author of evil and tries to reconcile it some with his goodness. Yet, Grudem's language seems to ultimately make the same statement:

---

39. Calvin, *Institutes*, 136.
40. Calvin, *Institutes*, 136.
41. Calvin, *Institutes*, 136–37. Interestingly, this includes the violence of the Old Testament.
42. Rigney, "Confronting the Problem(s) of Evil," *Desiring God*, https://www.desiringgod.org/articles/confronting-the-problems-of-evil.
43. Grudem, *Systematic Theology*, 323.
44. Grudem, *Systematic Theology*, 323

without God's involvement, evil does not occur. If God must be involved in some capacity for evil to occur, then he is behind it. This is a stark contrast to Young's definition of God's goodness, and emphasis on human free will as the explanation for why evil exists. For Young, God's only involvement with evil is in using it for good. For Calvin, Rigney, and Grudem, God is much more heavily involved in evil. Yet, it must be considered whether or not God can remain innocent while being behind evil in any manner. Young would undoubtedly answer the statement with a resounding "No!" For Young, darkness has no place in light just as lies have no place in truth. One cannot ever state that murder, child rape, incest, or any other sin, is orchestrated by a good God. To say such is to conclude that God's definition of good is so other to humanity's conception of good that too far a proverbial bridge exists across the massive valley of uncertainty. Such a bridge, it seems, Young is not willing to cross.

ENCOUNTERING YOUNG

Young's emphasis on free will seems genuinely helpful when discussing the problem of evil. When reading Young, there is no confusion as to whether or not God is behind tragic events and evil. Humanity is behind such things, and presumably, nature if we include other tragic disasters. But these are not the result of God's direct action. For Calvin and those impacted by his writings, such a view is problematic when defining the precise nature of sovereignty. For the Calvinist, sovereignty means overt control of all actions and events. For Young, however, sovereignty is seen in the relinquishing of control by God, and the submission of God to the choices of his creation. And most importantly, to God's redemption of those choices that arise from independence and darkness. This is divine sovereignty for Young. This is divine goodness.

Young has contributed significantly to the conversation about the nature of God's goodness. He has, without providing an in-depth analysis, laid a foundation for conversation about the goodness of God, and how this goodness impacts our view of Scripture.

The God Who is Light

This seems to be a conversation that Scripture itself is willing to have with the reader. We see Jesus healing people and loving people, and then proclaiming that he is only doing that which he sees his Father doing (John 5:19). The text even states boldly that Jesus cannot do anything without first seeing the Father do it. This suggests that God was acting in such a way before Jesus even mirrored his actions. In other words, Jesus did not make God the Father a nicer deity through his incarnation: Jesus incarnated the very goodness of God and expressed it in the human context. This reality is also seen in John 1 wherein God the Son, the *logos*, is said to offer "grace upon grace" from the very core of his being (John 1:16, NASB). This verse mesmerizes me. The text says that believers have received "grace upon grace" out of his own "fullness" (NASB). The meaning behind these subtle words is easily glossed over. The Word, the *logos* or exact expression of God or message of God, has grace before he even incarnates! It makes up his "fullness" or "wholeness," the pure contentment he has within himself. He lacks nothing, and grace comes from this abundance. Grace is not an afterthought of God. Grace does not exist because of sin. Grace is part of the genetic makeup of God that has always been flowing out of his fullness. What Jesus did was bring this grace in the most tangible way possible. Jesus does what the Father has always done, and Jesus offers what God has always been. Young seems to recognize these realities in his writings about God's goodness: there is no God but the God of Jesus. This God is light and "in him is no darkness at all" (1 John 1:5, ESV). He cannot be, in action, what he is not. The key, however, is in determining if humans can discern all the possible ways that God expresses his goodness. To be sure, we cannot for we are finite creatures. There remains, therefore, the possibility that God can act in a way that we do not understand. To this I'm sure even Lewis would concede. We are humans and he is God. Yet, as highlighted by Young, we ought to begin with Jesus as we seek to understand precisely what was happening in various Old Testament passages that depict often horrendous violence, or as we discuss the problem of evil, or even encounter the problem of evil in our own lives. At the very least we can say that love is

A Love in the Key of Three: The Triune Community

predictable and that it will look a certain way and not another way. Love will look like the fruits of the Spirit. Love will look like Jesus.

Young takes previously established conversational lines and embeds them into story. This blending of story with important theological ideas creates conversations because it forces Young's readers to not look at ideas such as God's goodness in a detached form, but rather in a relational manner which humanizes, if such a word can be used, these implications. What are we to conclude, as God's creatures, if he is the author of evil? Can such a God be trusted? Would Mack choose relationship with such a God if he discovered that God actually did directly influence Missy's murder? Would Lilly have overcome her shame if she knew that such a God authored her sexual abuse? Would Tony have ever climbed the proverbial mountain of chaos and plunged into the ocean of relational grace, if God had killed his son through cancer? In Young's mind, and certainly to those who have encountered deeply the love of God, the answer is an incontrovertible no. The absurdity of trusting such a God is brought out clearly in Young's works as these complex concepts are brought into the context of the actual lives of his characters which in turn forces the reader to cross the bridge into knowing God in their own lives and circumstances. I think of my own life circumstances: childhood abandonment which left threads of shame and unworthiness that I've had to face with God knowing that he was not the one who neglected me; vile illnesses which follow my family members around on a daily basis, a conscious decision present to not blame God; a tumultuous cultural climate full of darkness that I can only say is not anything like God; and personal struggles with sin and the flesh which must be utterly divorced from who God is in his being. Are these from God? Could they be if he were good? Young's works force us to make a decision about such things in a way that mere theological musings rarely can.

CHAPTER 5

THE GOD WHO WANTS TO BE KNOWN

Encountering Young's Mysticism

YOUNG'S FOCUS ON THE RELATIONAL Trinity is a strong theological current that weaves through all of his beliefs and writings. This first part has sought to establish this current in an exploration of the nature of the Trinity, showing that Young builds the entirety of his theology from the triune existence of God. The next part seeks to explore further the nature of the Trinity as it directly impacts humanity within its spiritual condition and context taking care to focus on the spiritual condition of humanity as it relates to the atoning work of Christ. In bringing part 1 to a close, and forming the foundation for part 2, it is critical to reiterate that all of Young's theology, whether it be about the innate relational existence of the Trinity, or about God's relation to humanity, is founded upon the concept of encounter. God has been encountering himself in an eternal love affair for eternity and has created humanity to encounter him through relationship. The concept of humanity

A LOVE IN THE KEY OF THREE: THE TRIUNE COMMUNITY

encountering God also goes by the theological label known as mysticism. A brief exploration of Christian mysticism will provide the foundation for humanity's interaction with the triune God discussed in part 2.

DEFINING MYSTICISM

While mysticism as a term is, perhaps, not easy to define, it is unmistakably founded upon the concept of encountering God.[1] Elwell argues that virtually all forms of mysticism exist to achieve this encounter, often called union. According to Elwell union is often achieved through some form of extreme contemplation or purgation (actions to eradicate the sin nature).[2] The experiences which arise from these practices are then expressed by mystics through imagery and metaphorical writing though such expressions are usually viewed as imperfect articulations of the experience.[3] It may be said, therefore, that mysticism is the practice of encountering God and then exerting effort to communicate about this encounter to the world.

According to scholar Bernard McGinn, Christian mysticism is also "rooted in the reading of the Bible."[4] This reading, however, is not designed to cultivate an "academic understanding of

---

1. McGinn, *Christian Mysticism*, 3. McGinn argues that the term was originally used, in Greek and Latin (Greek: *mystikos*; Latin: *mysticus*), to often refer to the secret practices of the mystery cults though it came to be used widely within the Christian context to speak of a mystical meaning of a particular scriptural text. This particular use is seen in Origen's writings. See Origen, *First Principles*, 333–417. See also Elwell, *Evangelical*, 806–7. According to Elwell, throughout church history mysticism has existed in different forms from movements emphasizing silent contemplation to rituals designed as purgatives for the soul that the individual may find union with God. Thus, mysticism was not only a way of viewing Scripture, as argued by McGinn, but there was always an experiential aspect to it.

2. Elwell, *Evangelical*, 807.

3. Elwell, *Evangelical*, 807.

4. McGinn, *Christian Mysticism*, 3. This biblical emphasis is sometimes called "scriptural mysticism," 35.

The God Who Wants to Be Known

the scriptural text."[5] According to McGinn, the mystic is also not interested in "a repository of doctrine and moral regulations."[6] Instead, the mystic desires to "penetrate to the living source of the biblical message, that is, the Divine Word who speaks in and through human words and texts."[7] This penetration into encounter with God results in the "transformation of the self based on a new understanding of the human relation to God."[8] The transformation of the self is, interestingly, often the cause of encounter with God, and also the result. In the works of St. John of the Cross, for example, self-denial resulting in change, is a prerequisite for gaining union with God. St. John calls the state of purgation "the dark night": "This dark night is a privation and purgation of all sensible appetites for the external things of the world, the delights of the flesh, and the gratifications of the will."[9] As he states further, individuals must journey towards union with God by depriving "themselves of their appetites for worldly possessions."[10] In this conception of mysticism there exists a proverbial ladder to climb in which the individual readies himself or herself for an encounter with God which in turn transforms them.

According to McGinn, mysticism also often emphasizes the importance not of encountering God in some ambiguous or obscure sense, but rather, encountering the Trinity as Father, Son, and Spirit.[11] One of the most beautiful expressions of this form of mysticism is found in the writings of Mechthild of Magdeberg (1208 A.D.–1282 A.D.). Her revelations about the Trinity seem as

5. McGinn, *Christian Mysticism*, 3.
6. McGinn, *Christian Mysticism*, 3.
7. McGinn, *Christian Mysticism*, 3.
8. McGinn, *Christian Mysticism*, xiv.
9. St. John, *Collected Works*, 119. Asceticism and purgation were also present in theologians such as Athanasius of Alexandria, Evagrius Ponticus, James of Vitry, and Catherine of Genoa. See McGinn, *Christian Mysticism*, 191-472 for a thorough account of this.
10. St. John, *Collected Works*, 120.
11. McGinn, *Christian Mysticism*, 191. This form of mysticism arose to prominence especially starting between A.D 200 and 400 when the theological articulation of the Trinity began to develop.

though they could have been written by Young himself. During one of her revelations, for example, she encounters the inner council of the Trinity as they decide to make humanity. The Son and the Holy Spirit say to the Father: "let us make man in our image and likeness (Gen 1:26). Even though I foresee the great miseries to come, I will still love man with everlasting love."[12] The Father answers: "The internal sweetness of your love, O Son, touches me; I will not hold back my feelings from you for the sake of love. Therefore, we will become fruitful by creating so that we can be loved in return and so that the greatness of our majesty may be acknowledged in some small way, I will prepare for myself a bride."[13] Then, quite poignantly and powerfully, the Son speaks these loving words to the Father: "Father, you know that I finally will die for love, but still joyfully we wish to make this creature in great holiness."[14]

I have little doubt that Young and Mechthild would have been instant friends should they have lived at the same time. Mechthild communicates both an intimate relationship existent between the members of the Godhead, and also an eternal unity of love directed towards humanity. The personal language she uses, especially of the Son, expresses a love that moves to action despite knowing the cost that it will pay for the sake of relationship. This language takes the concept that "God is love" and breathes life and action into it that love may be seen as a relationship of self-sacrifice. What immediately comes to my mind is the segment of *The Shack* in which Papa and Jesus are said to share the same scars from the crucifixion.[15] This is very clearly a text about the intimate relationship between the Son and the Father, a relationship in eternal consummation through union. The Father and the Son, as in Mechthild's words, are portrayed as having made a decision to create despite the pain that would ensue because of this decision. Similarly, it is not difficult to imagine Mechthild's words being expressed during the creation account in *Eve* where three voices dance and sing

12. Mechthild of Magdeberg, "Flowing Light," 204.
13. Mechthild of Magdeberg, "Flowing Light," 204.
14. Mechthild of Magdeberg, "Flowing Light," 204.
15. Young, *Shack*, 96–97.

The God Who Wants to Be Known

creation into existence.[16] Young's account of creation as a joyous and jubilant expression of love is made even more poignant knowing that God understood that his own creation would eventually crucify him. Love always takes these significant risks in Young's works, all in the name of encounter.

While the parallels between Young and Mechthild's trinitarian mysticism are obvious, Young seems quite distant from other forms of mysticism such as forms that encourage purgation or asceticism.[17] All of Young's characters encounter God within themselves without any demand on the part of God for them to perform some type of action to take part in these intimate encounters. God never demands that his creation perform any type of works in order to somehow earn an encounter with him. Furthermore, as will be discussed in the following chapters, Young is quite clear that just as there is no point in time when the Trinity has been fractured relationally, there is no separation between humanity and God. Humanity was born at the center of God's love and presence, and always continues its existence at the very center of his all-encompassing love. Union, therefore, is not something that is achieved in any manner of speaking: it is a free gift emanating from God's love. Therefore, mysticism, for Young, is certainly about an encounter with God yet it is an encounter that is not earned or achieved. Rather, the encounter is a constant, a reality, which surrounds humanity at all times though humanity can choose to not participate in it. Human volition is central to Young's understanding of the human side of encounter. God cannot keep his presence from anyone: outside of God is non-being, as Young observes.[18] However, God does not force relationship on any person. This is absolutely fundamental to understanding Young's view of human participation in relationship with God. God honors and

---

16. Young, *Eve*, 16.

17. Purgation is the practice of getting rid of the sin nature through various religious acts. Asceticism is related to this and is focused on depriving oneself of various pleasures in life for the sake of becoming more holy. For a response to this form of spirituality, see Farley and Chalas, *Perfect You*, 33–80.

18. Young, *Lies*, 131–64.

respects humanity's decisions to such a major degree that he does not force himself or his will on anyone.[19] However, he gives himself constantly to people. How can he not? He is life itself. If he wants humanity to live, then it must forever stay inside of his presence. Young's mysticism is about a relational encounter with God but without climbing any ladder. It was God who climbed down the proverbial ladder to Mack, Tony, and Lilly. God met them in the center of all of their failures and tragedies and asked nothing in return! It was this acceptance, this encounter with God's triune love, that ultimately changed each character.

COMPARING YOUNG AND THE MYSTICISM OF ST. JOHN OF THE CROSS

Despite their radically different expressions of mysticism, a parallel exists between Young and St. John of the Cross. This continuity can be seen in St. John's *The Living Flame of Love*. The work describes the experience of the soul that has achieved the union with God desired in *The Dark Night of the Soul* and the process towards the union outlined in *The Ascent of Mt. Carmel*. In both works, St. John speaks of the necessity of self-denial to achieve union with God. *The Living Flame of Love* describes the experience of actually achieving this union. Two selections from the work help to illustrate the parallel. First, St. John describes God's love as a "living flame of love that tenderly wounds my soul in its deepest center."[20] In his commentary on the poem, St. John states that the living flame of love is the Holy Spirit.[21] The Holy Spirit, who is the essence of God's love within the soul, "wounds the soul with the tenderness of God's love, and it wounds and stirs it so deeply as to make it dissolve in love."[22] Here St. John is describing the union that has been achieved through the process of

---

19. Young, *Lies*, 40.
20. St. John, *Collected Works*, 63.
21. St. John, *Collected Works*, 641.
22. St. John, *Collected Works*, 643.

The God Who Wants to Be Known

asceticism and purgation spoken of in his other writings. For St. John, this wounding of the soul seems to be metaphorical for he states that there is no more purgation left to achieve because the soul has achieved union.[23] St. John seems to be using this language to express the perpetual power of God's love upon the soul even after it has been sanctified. Young also seems to view God's love as wounding in his own context however this "wounding" is genuine healing of the soul through the healing of each person's independence from God. For example, in *The Shack*, Mack's forgiveness of the Ladybug Killer was the result of Mack knowing God's love for himself. When Mack chooses to forgive Missy's killer, there is an immense amount of pain that occurs.[24] In fact, it is such an intense pain, such a difficult task, that Mack has to say the words "I forgive you" multiple times.[25] For Young, God's love is not passive: it is always seeking restoration and healing. As we've discussed, Young takes major issue with the idea of God's love wounding individuals in a violent or abrasive manner (he is always good). To the contrary, God's love is submissive and expressed through servitude. However, through this servitude and participation in relationship with humanity, God's love reveals truth and truth often hurts Young's characters as it inherently reveals these characters' wrong relation to it. God's love seeks to "wound" in such a way as to cause a return to truth that heals the soul. To be sure, St. John has a different concept in mind. However, his description of God's love expressed through the Holy Spirit has an undeniable power that is clearly paralleled in Young's framework.

Another significant selection from St. John's work is worth mentioning: "How gently and lovingly you wake my heart, where in secret you dwell alone; and in your sweet breathing filled with good and glory, how tenderly you swell my heart with love."[26] St. John portrays this experience as occurring at the proverbial top of a spiritual ladder. Yet, such language is reminiscent of Young's

---

23. St. John, *Collected Works*, 643.
24. Young, *Shack*, 224–27.
25. Young, *Shack*, 227.
26. St. John, *Collected Works*, 640.

views of a divine love that has been believed and trusted by his creation. For Young, this love is not only for the elite Christian, as one could say St. John seems to believe. To the contrary, it is for the one who *dares* to encounter it. Those who do encounter God's love do not necessarily bring themselves into union with this love in an ontological manner as if there was a genuine distance between the individual and God. However, there does exist a relational union with love in Young's writings that occurs at the moment the individual responds to this love.[27] Those who respond certainly have hearts that "tenderly" swell with God's love. The change that occurs when one encounters God's love is seen in all of Young's works as will be demonstrated in part 2. This change causes the person's heart to so swell with love, in fact, that it overflows into the hurting world.

COMPARING YOUNG AND THE MYSTICISM OF BRENNAN MANNING

Moving into a more contemporary setting, parallels exist between Young's understanding of encounter and that of late theologian and mystic, Brennan Manning. This parallel is expressed clearly in Manning's definition of religion: "Religion is a matter, not of learning how to think about God but actually encountering him."[28] Manning's own encounter with Jesus happened at a Franciscan chapel in Loretto, PA. Manning was about to abandon his aspirations of becoming a Franciscan priest but found his leave of the monastery delayed when he decided to go to the chapel for a few minutes to pray.[29] Manning stayed on his knees in front of the twelfth station, the one depicting Jesus's crucifixion, in prayer for three hours during which time he encountered what he calls "infinite love."[30] This is the moment that became the foundation for all of Manning's

---

27. Young, *Shack*, 149.
28. Manning, *Relentless Tenderness*, 17.
29. Manning, *Relentless Tenderness*, 39.
30. Manning, *Relentless Tenderness*, 38.

writings and spiritual life. For Manning, life became about believing, in the deepest recesses of the heart, that we are loved by God. Even spiritual practices, such as prayer, became about "letting ourselves be loved by God."[31] This love, Manning states, is "based on nothing, and that fact that it is based on nothing makes us secure. Were it based on anything we do, and that 'anything' were to collapse, then God's love would crumble as well."[32] Yet, such is not the case for the God of Manning or Young. Both thinkers believe in a love from God that emanates from the core of God's nature, a love that is absolutely free and independent of human action. Both thinkers also maintain passionately the necessity of *knowing* this love, not just intellectually, but relationally.

ENCOUNTERING YOUNG

In Young's works, encounter with this love, and not religious rules and regulations, is what leads to changed lives. For Young, this love in the key of three, this otherworldly and utterly supernatural love, originated within the eternal Trinity, led to the creation of humankind, and was expressed perfectly in the person and redemptive work of Jesus. This is the metanarrative of Christianity for Young: love has always been and will always be. Our trust in this love does not make it real for if it did, then, as Manning would say, God's love would collapse upon the rubble of our faithlessness. To the contrary, this love only needs to be encountered through trust and relationship. This relationship emanates from the very nature of love itself for God is a relationship of love and created humanity to partake in his trinitarian existence. Humanity simply encounters this love and allows itself to be changed by this love. This is the essence of Young's mysticism: an encounter with ever-present, unconditional love.

Young's emphasis on encountering God reflects the metanarrative of Scripture from Genesis to Revelation. God is always

---

31. Manning, *Relentless Tenderness*, 31.
32. Manning, *Relentless Tenderness*, 22.

desirous of the hearts of his creation. Eternal life, for example, is described as knowing the Father and the Son (John 17:3). Eternal life is not independent of relationship. To the contrary, a marriage exists between the two concepts. Jesus describes himself as "the way, and the truth, and the life" (John 14:6, NASB) and the "resurrection, and the life" (John 11:25, KJV). Jesus and eternal life are inseparable. Because eternal life is a person, and not strictly speaking an intellectual assertion or doctrine, this person cannot be merely intellectually known. We are not saved by a belief in some theological concept: we are saved by a person. This person must be known for salvation to be known. God did not need to create humanity: he lacked nothing. The purpose that remains for God's creating people is relationship. God's promise to Abraham was even delivered in the form of relationship. Abraham did not believe in some abstract concept: he believed God and became righteous as a result (Gen 15:6). His belief in God came from encounter. In Jeremiah, God makes no small mention of Israel's history of choosing other gods to serve besides the one true God (Jer 16:11). Assertions from God like this one are highly relational in nature. As much as Israel was required to live in a religious system, it seems that this system really was a means to an end meant to be replaced by the New Covenant of Christ (Heb 1, 8, 10) which is founded upon relationship. Young's decision to make relational encounter with God primary for his framework is quite biblically appropriate indeed.

PART 2

WHEN LOVE MEETS THE BROKEN
The Healing Work of God

"Experience is a force not easily discounted."
EVE IN *EVE*

CHAPTER 6

THE CONDITION OF HUMANITY

THERE EXISTS A MYRIAD OF ways that humanity has been viewed theologically throughout the centuries. For example, the Calvinist framework highlights this issue in significant distinction from Young. Is humanity so far enmeshed in sin, so enslaved to its power, that it cannot choose God? The Calvinist framework suggests so. For theologians like John Calvin, humanity is utterly dependent on God's preemptive, regenerative, action upon the individual for without this humanity is lost in sin and unable to believe in Jesus.[1] Calvin has, what Young would undoubtedly say, a *low* view of humanity.[2] Young has called such theology P.O.S. theology on multiple occasions because of his strong aversion to it.[3] For Young, P.O.S. theology is connected deeply to the concept of shame ("There is something wrong with me") and is based upon an incorrect understanding of humanity's innate relation to God. According to Young, in clear unity with his foundation of trinitarian love, sin has never caused a separation between God

---

1. See especially Calvin, *Institutes*, 146–95.

2. Here "low" view is not a value statement so much as an indication of humanity's innate goodness or ability to choose God.

3. See Young, "You Never Need to Feel Shame," https://wmpaulyoung.com/feel-shame/. P.O.S. theology is "piece of shit" theology.

and humanity.[4] It simply is not powerful enough to accomplish such an act. There exists, instead, a *perceived* separation caused by humanity's decision to live independently from God.[5] For Young, the human condition is not one of innate badness but rather innate misunderstanding as to the nature of God, and the nature of humanity.[6]

This misunderstanding regarding separation is certainly powerful for people even if it is only a perception. In *Eve*, for example, Lilly often uses language that speaks of her perceived unworthiness for God's love, and presumably, his presence.[7] This arises out of her own broken heart caused by the sexual assault she endured.[8] In *The Shack*, Mack often feels abandoned by God because of his tragic

4. Young, *Lies*, 225.

5. Young, *Lies*, 232.

6. Young's view has some parallel to Irenaeus's understanding of original sin. See Irenaeus, *Against Heresies*, 496, 498. Irenaeus argues that original sin is the result of humanity's immaturity: "But created things must be inferior to Him who created them, for the very fact of their later origin; for it was not possible for things recently created to have been uncreated. But inasmuch as they are not uncreated, for this very reason do they come short of the perfect," 496. Irenaeus certainly believed that God could create a perfectly matured creature. However, he states that humanity was not able to receive a perfect nature for they were intentionally made infantile, by God, and needed a maturation process, 497. Irenaeus believed that this maturation process occurred through identification with Christ's own maturation process: "It was for this reason that the Son of God, although He was perfect, passed through the state of infancy in common with the rest of mankind, partaking of it thus not for His own benefit, but for that of the infantile stage of man's existence, in order that man might be able to receive Him," 497. Thus, humanity is to progress "towards the perfect" through daily obedience to Jesus, 498. For further interaction with this view, see Hick, *Love of God*, 214–15. Young does not present humanity as immature as though made so by God. However, he does present humanity with a certain vulnerability that Irenaeus would perhaps appreciate. This vulnerability is seen in humanity's misunderstanding of the nature and presence of God caused by sin.

7. See Young, *Eve*, 34, 51, 66 for examples of this in the work.

8. Young, *Eve*, 46. Young often speaks of his own sexual assault at the hands of tribal people during his time as a missionary child in New Guinea. The assault continued at the boarding school he was sent to by his parents. For a detailed account see Kris Wolfe's interview of Wm. Paul Young, "Childhood Sexual Abuse," https://www.youtube.com/watch?v=yTCCsuLw-Dc.

The Condition of Humanity

life experiences (his father's physical abuse and Missy's murder).[9] The anger expressed by Mack regarding both cases seems to arise out of some sense of shame. Yet the myriad of feelings, as much as they influence Young's characters, do not speak the reality of their proximity to God, or even their relation to God.

While not every person is in right relationship with God, in Young's theology, every person is a child of God.[10] Young does not affirm this to the exclusion of the importance of belief in Jesus. For Young, the action of faith is the decision to believe, in a subjective manner, what is true absolutely.[11] Young is not saying that all people are merely made in the image of God as if this concept is separate from the notion of becoming God's child through faith in Jesus. He affirms that being made in God's image is synonymous with being God's child.

Young argues that this universal familial inclusion is expressed in Scripture. A key section for Young is Acts 17:26–29 (NASB). The text states that God made "from one man every nation of mankind" and placed them in certain locations that they might "feel around for Him and find Him." The text then goes on to suggest that all humanity is "His descendants." Young highlights Paul's use of the word "descendants" arguing that it assumes the universal inclusion of humanity into God's family.[12] This verse also speaks in favor of Young's view on the closeness of God to humanity for "He is not far from each one of us." It could be said, therefore, that Young in fact believes that the knowledge of one's

---

9. See Young, *Shack*, 78. Mack's angry prayer to God about Missy's death expresses his perception of both God's nature and his own proximity to God. See also 160 and 161 where Mack's reflections about his own childhood abuse cause anger to rise within him.

10. Young, *Lies*, 206. For a direct criticism of Young's view see James B. De Young's work, *Exposing*, 30–34. De Young seems to misunderstand Young's assertions about universal familial inclusion. He does not address the difference between an ontological distance between humanity and God, and an existential "distance" in Young's writings. De Young's criticism is analyzed extensively in the appendix of this work.

11. Young, *Lies*, 205.

12. Young, *Lies*, 206.

identity, what he calls "the truth of our being,"[13] is not far from any person and needs only be touched to be received. It is atop this foundation that Young builds his understanding of sin.

Young argues that the nature of human sin can best be understood through an analysis of the Greek term, *hamartia*. In fairly typical fashion, Young concludes that the word means to "miss the mark."[14] Yet, this is not speaking primarily of missing a moral standard though his view does not completely rule this out. Rather, Young believes the term speaks of missing the truth of one's identity as God's child.[15] This seems to be a condition into which humanity is born, however, in Young's works, it is often life circumstances that highlight the sin condition. In *Cross Roads*, for example, Tony is clearly missing the mark through a lack of trust and relationship with God, and connected to this, a lack of understanding his identity as God's child. Tony's misunderstanding of his identity is seen in his constant self-abasement and self-centered lifestyle which included divorcing his wife, then intentionally winning her back only to divorce her again.[16] Tony's relationship with his daughter is also noticeably strained because of his actions.[17] The example of Tony, and of Lilly and Mack above, demonstrate the dire condition in which humanity finds itself according to Young. God is near all people, and all people are God's children. This is the first critical component to understanding Young's view of humanity. Yet simply because God is near all people, and all people are God's children, does not mean that there are not significant consequences for sinful decisions. Young is very clear on the impact that sin has on individuals, and by extension, families. Young's own personal encounter with God happened during his own existential crisis arising out of his affair.[18] The events of *The Shack* are based upon the

---

13. Young, *Lies*, 228–29.

14. Young, *Lies*, 228.

15. Young, *Lies*, 228

16. Young, *Cross Roads*, 4. Tony is effectively described as a functioning alcoholic since the death of his son.

17. Young, *Cross Roads*, 4.

18. Young tells his story extremely frequently. See Binder, "'The Shack'

The Condition of Humanity

11-year healing journey that ensued from this as Young worked through his own hurt from childhood as well as the pain he had caused his wife. The Great Sadness, in *The Shack*, was effectively Young's own trauma and pain not only from childhood, but from his own actions.[19]

The Great Sadness is a common theme in all of Young's fiction works even if it is not directly mentioned. In *The Shack*, The Great Sadness is the death of Mack's daughter; in *Cross Roads*, it is the death of Tony's son;[20] and in *Eve* it is the sexual abuse experienced by the main character, Lilly.[21] Yet, these specific expressions of the Sadness are ultimately only reflective of the larger Great Sadness, the condition in which all humans find themselves: the sense of separation from God.[22] This sense of separation again, while only a *sense*, nevertheless has dire consequences for humanity. It seems, therefore, that aloneness is a key theological consideration for Young's view of humanity. The Trinity has never been alone, and therefore, is intrinsically community centric. Consequently, God cannot create anything that is healthiest when it is alone. The lie that one is alone, when believed, brings utter devastation to people's lives. God has said "yes" to humanity and continues to always say "yes." Humanity, however, often lives in the desolate "no" to God. This theme is paralleled in the theologies of George MacDonald and Karl Barth.

---

author talks about abuse, adultery and atonement," *Oregon Live*, www.oregonlive.com/faith/2015/05/the_shack_author_qa.html. See also Young, FGC 2016 Session 10, https://www.youtube.com/watch?v=K8fl_wprdck&t=9s.

19. Wolfe, "Childhood Sexual Abuse," https://www.youtube.com/watch?v=yTCCsuLw-Dc.

20. Young, *Cross Roads*, 4 and 234–36.

21. Young, *Eve*, 46.

22. Young, *Cross Roads*, 47. This is illustrated when Tony is talking to Jack about the nature of hell.

COMPARING YOUNG AND GEORGE MACDONALD'S UNDERSTANDING OF GOD AS FATHER

MacDonald believes that an incorrect understanding of one's relation to God as Father is the central crisis afflicting humanity: "The refusal to look up to God as our Father is the one central wrong in the whole human affair; the inability, the one central misery: whatever serves to clear any difficulty from the way of the recognition of the Father, will more or less undermine every difficulty in life."[23] For MacDonald, this refusal to acknowledge God as Father seems to be the seat of sin. Yet, MacDonald is not arguing that God is not already the Father of all. Rather, he sees humanity as not relating to him as Father. As he states, "He is our father, but we are not his children. Because we are his children, we must become his sons and daughters."[24] For MacDonald, God cannot become a father unless he already exists as a father for a "primary relation cannot be superinduced."[25] Whatever God is towards us from the beginning, he must always be for God cannot change. God cannot become something that he is not inherently within himself. Humans must, therefore, believe that they are children of God by origin, if they are to truly know God as Father. MacDonald rejects, in fact calls evil, any teaching that propagates the idea that God only is Father to those who believe the gospel.[26] With MacDonald, as with Young, there is a clear and eternal "yes" from God to humanity. God is the Father of all whom he creates. Yet, there is the possibility of resisting this "yes" through a rejection of God's fatherhood. MacDonald affirms that those who reject God as Father need to be born a second time, "from above," in order to have a right relation with God.[27] This seems to be what he has in mind by stating that God's children must become his "sons and daughters." Essentially,

---

23. MacDonald, *Unspoken Sermons*, 139.
24. MacDonald, *Unspoken Sermons*, 143.
25. MacDonald, *Unspoken Sermons*, 140.
26. MacDonald, *Unspoken Sermons*, 139.
27. MacDonald, *Unspoken Sermons*, 142.

The Condition of Humanity

humanity must become what it already is. Here there appears to be, as with Young, a difference between an ontological relation to God and an existential one. For MacDonald, there does not seem to be a way for humanity to not be part of God's family any more than a fish can live outside of water. Yet, there is an existential possibility of not relating to God as Father and experiencing the consequence of this decision.

COMPARING YOUNG AND THE ELECTION THEOLOGY OF KARL BARTH

A similar theme is found in Barth's work on election. For Barth, Jesus Christ is "the electing God."[28] This is Barth's effort to find the concept of salvific election upon, not an elusive or ambiguous God, but upon the very God of the Bible. There is no election, for Barth, apart from Jesus Christ who is God and Savior.[29] Barth also argues that Jesus Christ is the "elected man."[30] Jesus is not merely the God who elects, but also the conduit of humanity's own election and salvation. His salvation is so complete, so perfect, so sufficient, that there is no election outside of Him. With Barth, therefore, we see both perfect salvation through the electing God's decision to choose Jesus, as well as Jesus's perfect representation of, and association with, humanity. This view of election allows God to be both the subject of election (the electing God) as well as the object (the elected man).[31] The significance of this is found in God's eternal purpose of election. According to Barth, God's grandiose election is an affirmative "yes" towards the entirety of humanity, quite noticeably in contradiction to the view of election proposed by Calvin.[32] Whereas Calvin speaks of a limited atonement that is efficacious for all whom God has chosen, Barth

---

28. Barth, *Church Dogmatics II.*2, 145.
29. Barth, *Church Dogmatics II.*2, 145.
30. Barth, *Church Dogmatics II.*2, 145.
31. Barth, *Church Dogmatics II.*2, 146.
32. Barth, *Church Dogmatics II.*2, 28.

stands noticeably averse to such a conclusion for it is limiting of God's elective actions. Barth also stands against the unavoidable implication of such a view that God is an elector of the reprobate unto damnation. Barth, to the contrary, believes that election is incompatible with damnation. For Barth, election is an affirmative towards humanity, not an agent of condemnation. As Barth states, God "does not say No, but Yes."[33] Those who are eternally damned, therefore, damn themselves through a resistance to God's "Yes!" for as Barth says, to our "No He places His own nevertheless."[34] Those who resist this election, God allows to "perish beneath the hand which it has rejected but still cannot escape."[35] This hand, for Barth, is the love of God. Humans who reject God's love are in a state of opposition in which that love turns into humanity's own destruction in judgment and perdition. That is what the freedom of grace means for the creature towards whom it is directed."[36] For Barth there exists a reality and non-reality. Election is the purpose, the reality, of God's action towards humanity. Election is the fulfillment of God's love, not the "non-fulfilment" which is inherently not of God.[37] The human needs only participate in this fulfillment through living the "life ordained for it."[38] Herein exists tremendous parallel to Young's own conception of humanity's relation to God.

For Young, there is also not a "No" from God to humanity. There is no separation between God and his creation. There is only the affirmation. This has tremendous implications for Young's views of atonement and also hell and his corresponding *hope* for the salvation of humanity. If God is irreversibly disposed towards his creation and is unabashedly loving his creation and seeking union with it (which is the very necessary expression of his love), then there is never a distance between himself and humanity.

33. Barth, *Church Dogmatics II.2*, 32.
34. Barth, *Church Dogmatics II.2*, 32.
35. Barth, *Church Dogmatics II.2*, 32.
36. Barth, *Church Dogmatics II.2*, 32
37. Barth, *Church Dogmatics II.2*, 29.
38. Barth, *Church Dogmatics II.2*, 32.

The Condition of Humanity

Therefore, for Young, the condition of humanity is certainly one of brokenness. Yet, it is also, and most importantly, a condition of election to God's love.

ENCOUNTERING YOUNG

Young's views on humanity's condition are significant. He takes concepts previously established by theologians, such as MacDonald and Barth, and expresses them in union with the concept of trinitarian love. Humanity is forever loved because of the eternally unfolding trinitarian love of God, a love that has always been, and was unleashed imbedded in the very expression of creation. The brokenness of humanity is ultimately the result of a life of independence from God, a life of resisting its own election. Belief in Jesus does not result, therefore, in election, or even prove election for Young. Rather, as with MacDonald and Barth, it is a stepping into reality, an embracing of that which is already true. All who do not embrace reality continue a life of independence with a brokenness that is not on the mend, but rather, increasingly unfolding. To the contrary, those who embrace God's love for them and grab ahold of their election, become enveloped in the ever-unfolding love of God.

Young's use of Acts 17:26–29 is a wise decision for his argument. This passage certainly does speak of the relation that God has with all his creation, yet it also recognizes that there is a need for humanity to embrace God. I've often thought of the condition of humanity in this way: we are embraced by God from conception yet as one is embraced from behind. The decision we must make is to turn inwards, resting our heads upon his breast that we may receive the embrace and so be saved. This seems to be precisely what Barth, MacDonald, and Young are arguing, and what is represented in Acts 17:26–29.

Young's emphasis on humanity being made in God's image is also represented in Scripture. In the beginning, God makes humanity in their image (Gen 1:26–28). The plural use of "our" image is of course significant for it speaks of humanity's sharing in the triune image of God. Further on it seems, at least initially, that humanity loses this image after the fall: Adam has a child made in *his own* image, not overtly the image of God (Gen 5:3). However, quite significantly, the image of God in humanity is reaffirmed after the flood of Noah (Gen 9:6). In this passage, God is upholding the value of human life because humanity is made in God's *image*. Young seems to operate with this in mind. Sin, as disastrous as it is, does not eliminate the image of God in humanity. This provides the foundation for Young's understanding of the universal familial inclusion of humanity into God's family. Young believes that sin leads people to shame, or the belief that something is wrong with them when really, they are made in God's image and have infinite value. Young's assertions are value statements: sin does not remove the image of God and therefore the value of humanity. It must be said, however, that this in no way means that sin has not caused a serious condition to exist within humanity. Scripture is clear that something is "wrong" with humanity because of sin and humanity is consequently in need of salvation (Rom 3:23, Eph 1:13, Eph 2:1 for example). Young does not speak against this reality. He is simply rejecting shame, the idea that we are wrong at the core of our being. For Young, sin is, at best, a covering or sludge, over the beautiful diamond that exists at the core of each person. There seems to be room in Young's works, therefore, for humanity to recognize the impact that sin has had, while maintaining its need for spiritual healing and salvation. Young is not saying that everyone is whole or healed. He is saying that everyone is made in God's image and God wants to heal everything that distracts us from who we are. While Young's understanding of the human condition may deviate some from typical evangelical Christianity, there is still recognition of both the value of people and the need for Jesus. Young's emphases and ways of defining the human condition simply differ some from the mainstream of popular Christian culture.

While I agree with Young's emphasis on the value of humanity having been made in God's image, I believe in a firmer separation between believers and unbelievers than Young. When people believe, they are given a new "spirit" or "heart" that predisposes

The Condition of Humanity

them towards God (Ezek 36:26–27, Heb 8:10–12). This new heart and spirit sets them free from slavery to sin (Rom 6:18). I also differentiate between being children of God in a creation context, and children of God in the context of salvation. I think it is possible to have God as our Father in the sense of having been created by him, but still not be his children in the context of salvation. I'm convinced this adoption only occurs at faith in Christ (John 1:12). Young would likely affirm this view with the caveat that John 1:12 is speaking not of becoming a child of God ontologically, but existentially or experientially.

CHAPTER 7

Atoning Love

In order to understand Young's position on the atonement of Christ, his rejection of Anselm's satisfaction theory and penal substitution must first be understood: his current position is largely antithetical to these theories. Those who have not read much about atonement theory may be surprised to know that there are multiple theories as to precisely what Christ accomplished on the cross. The Socinian and moral–influence theories, for example, present the death of Christ as an expression of God's will for us to follow. With the Socinian theory, the life and death of Christ are presented as an example for the moral lives humans are to live. As Erickson states, a "beautiful and perfect example of the type of dedication we are to practice."[1] In this theory, the resurrection of Christ acts as a confirmation for the legitimacy of all Jesus's teachings by which we are to live.[2] The moral–influence theory takes the focus off Jesus as an example of humanity's obedience and instead presents the atonement as an expression or demonstration of God's love. This theory was promoted by Peter Abelard as a direct response to Anselm's view that the atonement was necessitated "by the fact that our sin

---

1. Erickson, *Christian Theology*, 716.
2. Erickson, *Christian Theology*, 716.

Atoning Love

is an offense against God's moral dignity and, consequently, there must be some form of compensation to God."[3] This view affirms that "Christ did not make some sort of sacrificial payment to the Father to satisfy his offended dignity. Rather, Jesus demonstrated to humanity the full extent of God's love for them. It was humans' fear and ignorance of God that needed to be rectified."[4]

Satisfaction theory and penal substitution are so similar they almost ought to be considered different nuances of the same theory. Erickson defines the satisfaction theory as Christ dying to satisfy the wrath of God towards sin.[5] In penal substitution, Christ is also presented as having taken God's wrath upon himself. Schreiner defines penal substitution as follows: "The Father, because of his love for human beings, sent his Son (who offered himself willingly and gladly) to satisfy God's justice, so that Christ took the place of sinners. The punishment and penalty we deserved was laid on Jesus Christ instead of us, so that in the cross both God's holiness and love are manifested."[6] The key difference between the two views is that the satisfaction theory sees sin as an afront to God's honor, whereas penal substitution sees it as a violation of God's moral law.[7] In penal substitution theory, Christ takes the punishment we deserve for our violation of God's law (substitution). In satisfaction theory, Christ takes the punishment we deserve for violating God's honor. In both cases, Christ is taking the punishment of the Father upon himself that humanity may be saved from the wrath of God.

Suffice it to say, Young's framework is not compatible with either view. Young does not see God as needing appeasement for any reason, be it for a violation of honor or of a moral law. Young's understanding of trinitarian love also forbids the notion that the

---

3. Erickson, *Christian Theology*, 717.
4. Erickson, *Christian Theology*, 717.
5. Erickson, *Christian Theology*, 727.
6. Schreiner, "Penal Substitution View," 67. For further discussion on the differences between the two theories see Sutherland, "From Satisfaction to Penal Substitution," 98–105.
7. Elwell, *Theology*, 118.

When Love Meets the Broken: The Healing Work of God

Father punished the Son on the cross for sin. Such a view is very problematic for Young for it violates his understanding of the love existent between the members of the Godhead.[8] Young argues that the cross was produced by a human system that has been influenced radically by violence.[9] This human system is punitive and juridical: when a sin is committed, there must be punishment (i.e. the cross). However, Young does not see God as working in this human way. God does not need to have his wrath satisfied in order to be able to forgive humanity, or initiate relationship with it. Instead, God chooses to forgive sin in the midst of humanity's crucifixion of his Son. This decision to forgive appears to have occurred in eternity before the creation of the world though it was manifested at the cross.[10] Forgiveness, therefore, is a decision made between the Godhead before sin even entered the world.

Young replaces the idea that the cross is juridical and punitive in nature with the concept that God took the most horrendous evil imaginable, the crucifixion of God's Son, and made it the revelation of his forgiveness of human sin, intimate love, and closeness to humanity.[11] Young views the cross, therefore, not as an instrument of divine justice, but rather of flawed human justice. This instrument that arose out of flawed humanity is then made into an instrument of healing. Young's view of atonement expands beyond a view that sees the death of Jesus as initiating God's forgiveness as would be seen in pagan conceptions of God. Instead, the cross, the most offensive evil especially as it is used in the murder of the Messiah, itself is transformed from a symbol of death to one of eternal life and divine grace. Because this seems to hold to a variation of Abelard's moral influence theory, we will call Young's view the healing model of atonement.[12] Young's healing model has

---

8. Young, *Lies*, 149.
9. Young, *Lies*, 150.
10. Young, *Lies*, 118.
11. Young, *Lies*, 153.
12. This is not a new term. For example, see Jersak, "Nonviolent Identification and the Victory of Christ," 31. Jersak uses the term to differentiate his views from more "juridicial" models of the cross. Jersak argues that the fall in

Atoning Love

in view two primary infirmities that plague humanity: the lie of separation,[13] and The Great Sadness that results from this lie.[14]

The lie of separation, or the belief that humanity is separate from God, is argued by Young to exist because of the incorrect belief that sin actually has the ability to overpower God's love.[15] Young maintains, however, that God's love is far more powerful than sin.[16] It is from this foundation that Young argues that separation is not ontological in nature but rather existential. Because humanity believes that it is separated from God because of sin it lives in a perceived condition of separation. This sense of separation is seen in Mack's personal perception of himself as being lost.[17] This is Mack's existential experience. He *feels* the sensation of lostness. Yet, Jesus reminds him that his location is not based on experience, but rather Jesus's own location and sense of belonging: Jesus is not lost, and therefore, neither is Mack.[18] The death, burial, and resurrection heals humanity of this incorrect belief. Young argues that all people were included in Jesus's death, burial, and

---

Genesis was not ultimately about disregarding God's law, but rather, the deception which occurred regarding God's essential nature. Consequently, Jersak believes that God did not separate Himself from humanity at the fall. Instead, God desired to change humankind's perception of himself through healing of the broken relationship between humanity and God. A component of this mission was the forgiveness of sins. As with Young, Jersak believes that this forgiveness of sins occurred during humanity's crucifixion of Jesus and acts as the 'antivenin' to Jesus's murder. Consequently, this forgiveness during such an act demonstrates God's true nature to humanity. See also Reichenbach, "Healing View," 117–56. Reichenbach, however, differs in his definition of the term. He seems to believe, unlike Jersak and Young, that a closer compatibility exists between God's so-called violent acts in the Old Testament, and humanity's healing, 122. He also holds a more juridical or punitive view of Jesus's suffering on the cross because he believes God punished Jesus, 128.

13. Young, *Lies.*, 230.
14. Young, *Shack*, 43–66.
15. Young, *Lies*, 225.
16. Young, *Lies*, 225.
17. Young, *Shack*, 114.
18. Young, *Shack*, 114.

When Love Meets the Broken: The Healing Work of God

resurrection.[19] This is the concept of ontological union. Before the foundation of time, humanity was included in Christ and therefore has never been separated from God.[20] The atonement of Christ expresses this union through God's realized closeness to humanity and his forgiveness of sin during the crucifixion.[21] This union is also expressed through Christ's own perceived separation from the Father for Christ experienced exactly what humanity experiences. Yet, for Christ, this was also an existential moment and not an ontological reality as seen in the shared scars between Jesus and Papa.[22] Unlike what is typically seen in satisfaction theory, or penal substitution, there is no sense of separation either between God and humanity or God and Jesus in Young's view.[23] Rather, there is God's effort to destroy the sense of separation through a heavenly invasion of earthly darkness.

The Great Sadness is intimately connected to the lie of separation. Because human's do not know who they are in relation to God (or where they are), there exists a spiritual hurt deep within the individual. In *The Shack*, The Great Sadness is described, in microcosm, as the loss of Mack's daughter Missy.[24] This Great Sadness in microcosm is also seen with Tony in *Cross Roads* as he recalls losing his son, Gabriel.[25] However, there does seem to exist a larger-scale Great Sadness within humans because of the lie of separation. This larger Sadness is also seen in *Cross Roads*. In the book, Tony is described as being a fairly unsavory individual largely because of his belief that he is separated from God.[26] This

---

19. Young, *Lies*, 119.
20. Young, *Lies*, 119.
21. Young, *Lies*, 119.
22. Young, *Shack*, 96.
23. See Grudem, *Systematic Theology*, 574. Grudem believes Jesus was separated from the Father on the cross. His explanation of this concept is representative of how penal substitution and satisfaction theories can be applied in this way.
24. Young, *Shack*, 43–66.
25. Young, *Cross Roads*, 4.
26. Young, *Cross Roads*, 3, 4, 49.

Atoning Love

separation has caused unloving and hurtful behavior to come from Tony which has caused alienation between he and his ex-wife and daughter.[27] At the conclusion of the book, Tony's conceptions of God are largely healed though no character of Young's seems to heal completely within their stories (we seem to see the foundation and beginning of their healing journeys).[28] Tony's healing from his ignorance about God's love also gives him the confidence he needs to face the loss of his son as well as come to an acceptance of the relational consequences of his abhorrent behavior.[29]

Young's work, *Eve*, stands as a very critical addition to his theology of humanity. Whereas *The Shack* and *Cross Roads* can be seen as "twin brothers" who share some similar settings and themes though with different applications, *Eve* is the adventurous and carefree daughter of the family creating her own path in life. This is not to say that *Eve* is completely different from the others, but that it explores The Great Sadness that exists in the heart of women, a setting that had not been previously explored in Young's work. In the book Lilly arrives in a strange in-between world presumably situated between Earth and Heaven. She arrives broken (literally) and battered from a life lived in the shadow of the "whisper of unworthiness" directed at her by the world.[30] This "whisper" was manifested in Lilly's life through her being trafficked at a young age.[31] This traumatic experience led her to believe that she was no prized possession of God, but rather, an object without intrinsic value.[32] Lilly's journey, unlike Mack's and Tony's, largely takes place in relation to the love of Eve and others who sought to heal her from the hurt of her past life.[33] The story is still very much about God's love for Lilly: on several occasions Lilly sees the love

---

27. Young, *Cross Roads*, 3, 4.
28. Young, *Cross Roads*, 233.
29. Young, *Cross Roads*, 233, 266.
30. Young, *Eve*, 66.
31. Young, *Eve*, 206.
32. Young, *Eve*, 206.
33. Young, *Eve*, 206, 40–44, 206.

of Eternal Man, or Adonai, and feels an instant attraction to it.[34] However, these relationships simply provide the tangible expression of God's love towards Lilly. In *Eve*, The Great Sadness is the belief of unworthiness that exists not only in Lilly, but women in general. Young seems to argue throughout the novel that women, from the beginning of the Fall, have been treated as objects in one way or another. Lilly is a direct image of this who, interestingly, finds healing through relationship, the very antivenom to unworthiness for relationship requires courage and vulnerability, traits that require a recognition of self-worth. It is security and safety inside of divine love in its various manifestations that brings each of Young's characters onto the healing journey.

In Young's theology, the cross is presented as the cure to humanity's wounded existence. The cross heals the lie of separation as Jesus becomes the epicenter of this lie in his own sensation, sensation of being separated from God on the cross. It also cures The Great Sadness. If God is love enough to die on the cross in the vicious manner in which he did, then he will stop at nothing to seek the inner healing of his entire creation. The cross, therefore, is not viewed by Young as a transaction to the Father: the cross is viewed as the location, much as is the case with Abelard, of the demonstration of God's love which penetrates the darkness of life. Here, again, Barth is helpful as an accentuation against which to view Young's understanding of atonement. For Barth, as discussed in the previous chapter, Jesus is God's "yes" to humankind. This affirmation assumes an eternal love which has been expressed perfectly in the person and work of Christ. Yet, this love can be resisted as in *Eve* (our "no" to his "yes"), or not believed as in *The Shack* and *Cross Roads*. This rejection or neglect of God's love leads to the lie of separation and, in Barth's language, the resistance to election. However, it does not alter, ontologically, the election itself.

---

34. Young, *Eve*, 45.

Atoning Love

COMPARING YOUNG AND GEORGE MACDONALD'S ATONEMENT THEOLOGY

Parallels exist between Young's and MacDonald's conceptions of atonement. MacDonald also rejects all forms of penal substitution or satisfaction theories of atonement. MacDonald does not view divine judgment as retributive in any manner. Rather, judgment is always restorative.[35] The cross, therefore, cannot be anything but restorative judgment. According to MacDonald, the closest we get to a juridical judgment in Scripture is the Old Testament sacrificial system. This system existed because Israel was not ready for God's revelation of love in Christ due to their past existence as a nation in slavery to Egypt. Israel would have been unable to receive such a concept in their context:

> Moses, the man of God, was not ready to receive the revelation in store; not ready, although from love to his people he prayed that God would even blot him out of his book of life. If this means that he offered to give himself as a sacrifice instead of them, it would show reason enough why he could not be glorified with the vision of the Redeemer. For so he would think to appease God, not seeing that God was as tender as himself, not seeing that God is the reconciler, the Redeemer, not seeing that the sacrifice of the heart is the atonement for which alone he cares.[36]

For MacDonald, God's tenderness and ability as a reconciler, are inherently opposed to a juridical view of atonement. God is, instead, interested in proving his love through the free forgiveness of sin (as with Young),[37] and in leading humanity to reject sin and consequently find healing from the human condition.[38] While God is unrelenting in his pursuit of humanity, individual people must choose to participate in relationship with God through the

---

35. MacDonald, *Unspoken Sermons*, 18.
36. MacDonald, *Unspoken Sermons*, 20–21.
37. MacDonald, *Unspoken Sermons*, 21.
38. MacDonald, *Unspoken Sermons*, 250.

rejection of sin and the choosing of righteousness: "Jesus came to deliver us. When we turn against them [sins] and refuse to obey them, they rise in fierce insistence, but the same moment begin to die. We are then on the Lord's side, as he has always been on ours, and he begins to deliver us."[39] MacDonald's language is reflective of God's eternal decision to call humanity his children (what Barth would call election) yet without participation this reality is not experienced by people. Unlike MacDonald, Young does not suggest that turning from sin is participation in relationship with God. Rather, in Young's works, turning from sin seems to be the result of participation with God and the healing of The Great Sadness. MacDonald's words place a higher emphasis on correct behavior as a mechanism for restored relationship with God than is present in Young. Young, however, focuses more on the individual's trust of God. The degree to which the individual trusts God is the degree to which the individual will find healing. This healing will positively impact behavior however right behavior is not the primary focus for Young.

ENCOUNTERING YOUNG

Young emphasis on the human origin of the cross is certainly appropriate from a historical perspective, as well as a biblical one. The cross was very much used by the Romans as an instrument of death, and there does not exist a place in Scripture that states that God *originated* the cross. On numerous occasions Scripture states clearly that Jesus was murdered *by humans* (Matt 20: 17–19; Matt 26:21–25; Luke 9:22; Mark 8:31; Matt 27:35; Mark 15:24; Luke 24:20; John 19:18; 1 Cor 2:8; Acts 2:36; Acts 4:10; Acts 5:30 to name just a few verses). In fact, Jesus does not once overtly say that his Father was going to kill him or murder him. This human side to the cross is undeniable in Scripture. The theological issue occurs in trying to make sense of how the human side is informed by the divine side, and *vice-versa*. Scripture does speak clearly,

---

39. MacDonald, *Hope*, 9.

Atoning Love

using different phrases, of God offering Jesus as a sin sacrifice (Isa 53:6; 53:10; Rom 8:3–4; John 3:16–17; 1 John 4:9; 1 John 4:14). Yet, there are also innumerable verses stating that Jesus offered himself for our sins (Gal 1:4; Heb 10: 12, 14; John 10:11). What Young's writing does is stir this theological pot that we may try and reconcile, with the power of the Holy Spirit, all these verses in a way that is honoring to the Trinity.

As for a potential resolution to this dilemma, I offer the following considering the challenging words offered by Young. What we see in the New Testament are four "levels" of understanding for the cross: 1) The Father gave the Son; 2) the Son gave himself; 3) Humanity killed the Son; and last, 4) Satan killed the Son (Luke 22:3). These verses, and so many, ought to create humility within us. As much as some aspects of the cross are clear (Jesus took away our sins) the precise mechanism behind this is quite mysterious. Forgiveness does seem to be a free decision of God in many places in the Bible. Jesus even forgives people before the cross (Matt 9:2, 6). This places a serious problem for proponents of penal substitution and satisfaction who argue that God *had* to send the Son for forgiveness to be given to humanity (as if our sins strongarmed God into this action). When Jesus is referred to as the sin offering, it is always in the context of the Old Covenant law, not the context of a divine truth that *had* to happen as if someone was holding a gun to God's head. In fact, the Old Covenant law is the only context in which the phrase "sin offering" makes sense. If we were to interpret this considering the pagan conceptions of deity, then Jesus could be seen as making a payment of sorts to the Father for forgiveness. However, this precise language does seem to be absent from Scripture. What God did he did in the context of *the law*. Jesus was a sin offering and God used the Law as the context for salvation. Furthermore, humanity was indirectly involved in this. As much as the Father gave the Son, and the Son gave himself, knowing full well what would happen, it was ultimately humanity, under the influence of Satan through Judas and others, that killed Christ, not the Father. The Father vindicated Christ by raising him from the dead (Acts 2:24). The irony of all of this is that Israel ultimately offered her own sin offering in the context of their sacrificial system. They demanded Jesus's death, and they got what they wanted, but God received it for humanity's salvation (I think of Israel chanting "His blood *shall be* on us and on our children!" in Matt 27:25, NASB).

I am more likely than Young to emphasize the mechanistic nature of this: *I believe Jesus did have to die for salvation.* I do not take this to mean that our sins strongarmed him into dying. Furthermore, I do not believe that the Father was an angry deity who needed pacification through blood. However, I am convinced that without this offering of Christ there is no forgiveness, not because God had to do it this way, but because this was the best way to prove his love (Rom 5:6–8). This emphasis seems to, in many ways, bypass the problematic language of penal substitution or satisfaction theories of atonement that do seem to present God in a more pagan manner (God *must* have blood to forgive). It also, in my view, potentially provides a reconciliation between Young's position where forgiveness is freely offered as a decision in the midst of Christ's crucifixion, and those positions that state the necessity of Christ's death for the divine offer of forgiveness. The Trinity decided that Jesus's death would be necessary for salvation in the context of the law so that the sinful darkness accentuated by the law may become the location of humanity's salvation, the ultimate "one-two punch" to the work of the enemy. This does not change the functional impact of the cross: Jesus died for us to have forgiveness and eternal life. Yet, it helps us to understand the nature of the death of Jesus and why this was required for forgiveness and salvation (Heb 9:16, 22).

This analysis proves the value of Young's work, not because it conforms to his own view, but because it shows how Young's thinking challenges our preconceptions about God, and forces us, if we allow it, to confront those passages that do contradict our views. For Young, the atonement of Christ is a direct expression of the trinitarian love of God. It is the simultaneous location of the most-vile expression of sin, and paradoxically, the fullest expression of God's love amid this sin. Young's rejection of more

Atoning Love

juridical forms of atonement, such as the satisfaction and penal substitution theories, forces the reader to consider whether such views could exist in harmony with the love shared between the members of the Trinity. Furthermore, Young seems averse to any form that treats Christ as a mechanism for forgiveness. If Christ is treated as such then the conclusion remains that God must have required this mechanism, which for Young, is a slippery slope down to the edges of more juridical views of atonement. Therefore, Christ's atonement on the cross is healing in nature for Young, not because it somehow earned this healing on behalf of humanity, but because Christ himself is expressive of the healing love of God: he is the healing love of God in the flesh. God, in his incarnation, became the earthly epicenter of divine love, seeking to heal the lies that have so broken humanity by becoming the very antithesis to this love on the cross and overcoming it through forgiveness and the revelation of God's proximity to humankind. This is the nature of the propitiation, for Young. God's intimacy with humanity is revealed and God's healing love is unleashed.

CHAPTER 8

HELL AND HOPE

THE CONCEPT OF HELL IS an issue that has often caused much theological friction especially when it is explored in light of God's love and grace. Hell is understood, generally speaking, as the final resting place, or condition, of the damned. All who have rejected Christ, find themselves in this torturous existence. Some theologians, and perhaps the majority of modern evangelicals, maintain that hell is some form of eternal conscious torment where God is either absent entirely or present in some form of judgment upon the unbeliever.[1] Others maintain that hell has a terminus: either through universal salvation,[2] or through the ultimate annihilation of the unbeliever, the existence of hell will cease at some future point.[3] In each of these conceptions of hell, the friction between God's love and grace, and the existence of eternal judgment, is revealed. If hell is an eternal separation from God, then tension exists between this idea and a God who is love and consequently seeks

---

1. For example, see Burk, "Eternal Conscious Torment," 17–43.

2. See Parry, "Universalist View," 101–27. See also Parry's work *Evangelical Universalist* written under the pseudonym of Gregory MacDonald.

3. For an excellent treatment of the overall topic of hell as it relates to God's love in general, and annihilationism, see Powys's monograph *Hell: A Hard Look at a Hard Question*.

Hell and Hope

union with his creation. Further tension exists when bringing this idea against God's omnipresence. Can God exist everywhere, *except* for hell? Or even more critically, can anyone exist apart from God who is life itself? The idea of post-mortem conversion creates tension between the justice of God and the love of God: is God just by allowing the salvation of all who are in hell? Does this not violate the very magnitude of their sins and grievances against him? Can such a God still be just? And with annihilationism: how are select passages which presumably speak of an eternal conscious torment to be understood if unbelievers will eventually, or perhaps instantly, be destroyed by God's judgment? Quite importantly, with all of these views, the particular mechanism of God's judgment must be defined. Is God punishing with his presence? Is he allowing Satan to torment people? Is he yelling at people in angry rage? And do any of his actions violate the fruits of the Spirit (Gal 5:22–23)? All these questions above express critical aspects of the concept of hell that deserve to be explored.

What makes Young's understanding of hell so fascinating, and in many ways, helpful in interacting with these questions, is that it also stems from the love of the triune God. God is love and has never been anything but love. Furthermore, this love is knowable by humans and does not contain any hidden "corners" that are inconsistent with the visible attributes of love seen in Christ. Whatever hell is, therefore, it must be an expression of God's love. This relationship between God's love and hell is what Young believes to be the central theological issue for the topic.[4] In Young's mind, hell cannot be a location that is not inhabited by God for God is everywhere.[5] Furthermore, God must inhabit hell because his creation is there and God cannot, because of his loving nature, ever abandon humanity.[6] It is from this foundational premise that Young frames the conversation about hell around two theological assertions.

---

4. Young, *Lies*, 132.
5. Young, *Lies*, 134.
6. Young, *Lies*, 134.

Young's first assertion is that if hell was not created by God, then it must have similarity to God himself who is also uncreated.[7] In this scenario hell would necessarily be part of God's non-created presence, and naturally as a result, a part of God's expression of love because he is inherently and eternally love.[8] If hell was somehow able to exist without God's willing it into existence, then hell would be innately related to the triune God of relational love. Young's second assertion is that if hell is part of God's creation then no created thing can ever separate an individual from God's love (Rom 8:38–39).[9] Whether hell is created or uncreated, it is an expression of God's loving nature. Perhaps it is no surprise, then, that Young views hell as not a place of punitive or juridical punishment, but rather, a place of God's healing presence expressed through love.[10] If hell is not separation from God and God's love, then there necessarily does not exist an end to God's mission to rescue humanity from sin and usher it into healing.[11] For Young, hell is ultimately the experience of God's love in the midst of human resistance to it.[12] Hell is, therefore, a continuation of, and magnification of, the human resistance of divine election.

Young's most prominent discussion in fiction about hell occurs in *Cross Roads*. As Anthony Spencer lies in a coma, he meets Jack, or C.S. Lewis.[13] Anthony is initially confused as to his surroundings and asks Jack if they are in hell. Jack replies: "Not exactly, at least not in the sense that you imagine it. I am certain Dante is not lurking nearby."[14] Anthony then describes his understanding of hell using language reminiscent of the eternal conscious

---

7. Young, *Lies*, 134.
8. Young, *Lies*, 134.
9. Young, *Lies*, 134.
10. Young, *Lies*, 134.
11. Young, *Lies*, 136.
12. Young, *Lies*, 136.
13. Young, *Cross Roads*, 43.
14. Young, *Cross Roads*, 43. Young's language here is an overt criticism of the infernalist language used by Dante in *Divine Comedy*.

Hell and Hope

torment view of hell.[15] Anthony believes that hell is a place where God punishes those who rebel against him.[16] He also concludes that hell is a place of separation from God.[17] In contrast to these views, the rest of the novel seems to define hell as a location, not in some obscure corner of the universe, but within Anthony's own soul.[18] Hell is, therefore, presented as an experience of the negative impact of sin, and the tragic events of Anthony's life, in the midst of God's loving pursuit of his healing. Because this experience occurs within Anthony's soul as he lays in a coma, Young seems to be suggesting the possibility that God's healing actions continue beyond what can be observed in natural existence. If God works supernaturally, then he is not confined or bound by anything in the natural.

Young also interacts with the concept of divine judgment in *The Shack*. Mack is asked by Wisdom to decide which of his five children to send to eternal damnation. Wisdom asks him to choose three while the other two are able to spend an eternity in Heaven.[19] Mack cannot ultimately make the choice and instead states that he'd rather be the one sent to hell.[20] Mack is then forced to interact with the implications of his decision as they relate to Missy's murderer.[21] Wisdom presents Missy's killer as the product of an abusive household (perhaps a reference to the killer's own Great Sadness) and in so doing, forces Mack to confront his own hatred of the Ladybug Killer.[22] Wisdom seems to be trying to encourage Mack to look at the world in the way God does. As Mack could not condemn any of his children, and instead volunteered to be sent to hell in their place, so God cannot condemn and instead sent Jesus to experience hell on behalf of humanity. Jesus experienced

15. Young, *Cross Roads*, 43.
16. Young, *Cross Roads*, 43.
17. Young, *Cross Roads*, 43.
18. Young, *Cross Roads*, 46, 286.
19. Young, *Shack*, 162.
20. Young, *Shack*, 163.
21. Young, *Shack*, 163.
22. Young, *Shack*, 163.

the *sense* of separation from God that all who are in opposition to his love experience. In this section, Young forces preconceptions about divine judgment to be exposed to the relational love of the Trinity. Judgment, in *The Shack*, is an extension of love for the sake of healing. God, it seems, is interested in healing the individual through this judgment which, in the broader story of *The Shack* and *Cross Roads*, seems to be defined as the resistance to God's love.

Young's view of hell as a place, not of separation from God, but rather of further experience of God's love, is the foundation for Young's *hopeful* universalism.[23] Christian universalism refers to the eventual, and total, salvation of all people through Christ. As Tom Greggs elaborates: "Christian universal salvation argues that in Scripture the atonement is an atoning for humanity and that Christ's objective work of salvation is effective for all human beings (not simply a select few by either election or exercise of freewill) by God who is the God of salvation."[24] This view as defined by Greggs is contrasted to pluralistic universalism in which humanity is not saved ultimately through Christ but simply through the will of an undefined God, as expressed by John Hick. Universalism is a dogmatic statement regarding the application of the atonement: all people will be saved through Christ. Hopeful universalism is different in nature.

Young's view of universalism as *hopeful* is critical to grasping his position. On one hand, Young has no issue declaring that

---

23. There are various possible labels for Young's position. See Jersak, "Why I'm not a Universalist," https://www.clarion journal.com/clarion_journal_of_ spirit/2019/09/harts-that-all-will-be-saved-i.html. Young has stated to me that he describes himself in the same manner as Jersak in this article: a proponent of ultimate redemption. Jersak argues that he has faith that all will be saved, though he cannot dogmatically say this. I argue that while Young does subscribe to this, the term hopeful universalist is helpful for this discussion as it takes into consideration Young's strong emphasis on human free agency. God has made a decision about humanity but will humanity respond? Young hopes so. I also believe that the term hopeful universalism is more clear an articulation of his beliefs for readers unfamiliar to the subject.

24. Greggs, "Christian Universalist View," 197.

Hell and Hope

all people have been saved in Christ.[25] Young maintains that our decision, as individuals, is to *participate* in our salvation or remain in the "blindness of our own independence."[26] God does not force this salvation on anyone. This would be unloving. Rather, God, because of his nature, continues to seek humanity, ushering it into relationship with himself, while leaving humanity the choice to say "yes" to his invitation, or "no." Young, understanding that people can continually reject God's love, demonstrates that he is decidedly not a universalist as Greggs defines the term, and as the term is mostly understood within historical Christianity. Young is not dogmatic about universalism: he does not say that all people will choose relationship with God and consequently *experience* salvation. In the simplest of terms, Young is not a universalist. However, he does maintain that God will never stop inviting people into this relationship while hoping for their right response to this invitation. This invitation is an expression of God's never-ending love, and it is this love that gives Young hope for humanity.

For Young, hell is the experience the unbeliever faces while in the presence of God. This presence is either a joy to those who believe in Jesus (what Young would likely call Heaven), or a torture for those who continue to resist his love and truth. Young's beliefs have continuity with several theologians who express universalistic themes: Origen, George MacDonald, and Hans Urs von Balthasar. Exploring Young's beliefs in comparison to these thinkers reveals that Young is working within a framework held by critical Christian theologians from the past, but he applies these themes in a nuanced hopeful manner.

YOUNG AND ORIGEN'S GOD OF LOVE

In most theological conversations about universalism, Origen is, perhaps, the name that first comes to mind when the topic of universalism in early Christianity is discussed. Origen's understanding

---

25. Young, *Lies*, 117–18.
26. Young, *Lies*, 118.

of universalism is founded upon a core foundation: the proximity of God's love to the unbeliever and the nature of the term, *apokatastasis*. Origen expresses his view of *apokatastasis* as follows:

> the end is always like the beginning; as therefore there is one end of all things, so we must understand that there is one beginning of all things, and there is one end of many things, so from one beginning arise many differences and varieties, which in their turn are restored, through God's goodness, through their subjection to Christ and their unity with the Holy Spirit, to one end, which is like the beginning.[27]

Origen defines *apokatastasis* as a return to the original intended reality of creation. Creation is restored through subjection to Christ's lordship. God brings people into this subjection through encounter with his love which purges the individual of sin.[28] The goodness of God is equated with the person of Jesus Christ who seeks to purify the sinner from sin that they may find salvation.[29] Origen further elaborates on this notion: "For the word is more powerful than all the evils in the soul, and the healing which is in him comes to be applied to each one in accordance with the very will of God, and the end of all things is for evil to be destroyed."[30] Origen's assertion that Jesus as the word is more powerful than evil is in alignment with Young's own thinking. As Young asserts throughout his works, sin never had the power to separate humanity from God.[31] Sin, therefore, does not have power over God in any manner. If sin cannot separate humanity from God, then sin can certainly not stop God from saving his creation. This all-encompassing love of God that seeks the purification, or in Young's works, healing, of humanity, even after death is a critical parallel between Origen and Young.

27. Origen, *First Principles*, 1.6.2, 71.
28. Origen, *First Principles*, 1.6.1, 70.
29. Origen, *First Principles*, 1.6.1, 70.
30. Harmon is quoting Origen, 'Contra Celsum 8.72', in Harmon *Every Knee Should Bow*, 52–53.
31. See especially Young, *Lies*, 225–34.

Hell and Hope

YOUNG AND GEORGE MACDONALD'S GOD OF FIRE

As has already been demonstrated in this work, Young and MacDonald have many theological threads in common. This is seen most clearly in their shared emphasis on God's purifying love. MacDonald, like Origen, believes God's love to be an unstoppable force that is forever exerted upon humankind. This love is purifying in nature:

> For love loves unto purity. Love has ever in view the absolute loveliness of that which it beholds. Where loveliness is incomplete, and love cannot love its fill of loving, it spends itself to make more lovely, that it may love more; it strives for perfection, even that itself may be perfected–not in itself, but in the object.[32]

For MacDonald, a direct correlation exists between the nature of God's love and the reception of this love by the individual. Love, it seems, is not fulfilled unless it is received. Judgment, therefore, is not juridical or punitive in nature: divine judgment is not about consignment to separation from God in hell. Rather, judgment is divine love's purification of the individual. MacDonald sees this reality in Heb 12:29, where God is described as a "consuming fire."[33] MacDonald believes that the passage speaks of a God who does not punish humanity due to a lack of "worship" but rather as a consuming fire that will "burn us until we worship."[34] Eternal punishment, for MacDonald, is ultimately God's action "to *destroy* sin" through his love.[35] MacDonald believes that all evil will ultimately be vanquished. At some future time even 'Death and Hell' will be thrown into the lake of fire that "Death shall then die everlastingly."[36] Here MacDonald uses noticeably strong language

---

32. MacDonald, *Unspoken Sermons*, 17.
33. MacDonald, *Unspoken Sermons*, 17.
34. MacDonald, *Unspoken Sermons*, 18.
35. MacDonald, *Unspoken Sermons*, 18.
36. MacDonald, *Unspoken Sermons*, 23.

suggesting the inevitability of universal salvation: God's love demands the salvation of all.

MacDonald uses stronger language than Young when speaking of God's purifying love. This language seems to suggest MacDonald's belief in the inevitability of universal salvation. Young is undoubtedly in agreement with MacDonald regarding the nature of love as a purifier of the individual, and the reality that this love never ceases even in a postmortem existence. Yet, Young cannot be considered a universalist at least not in the sense that one might consider MacDonald one. Young places too great an emphasis on God's willingness to allow humanity, of their own volition, to choose or reject him.

YOUNG AND THE HOPE OF HANS URS VON BALTHASAR

Perhaps the notion of a *hopeful* universalism is seen most clearly in von Balthasar. Von Balthasar holds two simultaneous convictions which comprise his hope: the reality of a divine punishment for sin, and the reality of the proximity of God's love in Christ to humanity in a post–mortem existence. These two sides of the same theological coin are quite formative for von Balthasar.

For von Balthasar, divine judgment is punitive in nature and acts as a judgment from God upon sinners.[37] The sheer severity of this judgment forces von Balthasar to have doubts as to whether or not humanity will ever be able to escape the judgment.[38] However, the severity of this judgment is balanced, for von Balthasar, with the notion that God, because of his immense love for humanity, has "born the sins of everyone."[39] These two aspects of von Balthasar's theology, the divine judgment of God and love of God, are what seem to keep him from making two ultimate and

---

37. Balthasar, *Dare We Hope*, 5.
38. Balthasar, *Dare We Hope*, 5.
39. Balthasar, *Dare We Hope*, 5.

Hell and Hope

conflicting assertions: that all humanity will eventually be saved, or that all humanity will be punished for eternity.[40]

In continuity with MacDonald, von Balthasar describes hell as the consuming fire of God's love.[41] For von Balthasar, the central question that arises from this assertion is whether hell will remain "stronger" than God's love.[42] Hell, therefore, seems to be the existence of humanity in opposition to God's love and in punishment for sin. Von Balthasar states further that "God does not damn anyone' but 'the man who irrevocably refuses love condemns himself."[43] There exists a tension even in his understanding as to the precise nature of hell. Is it a place of divine love? It certainly seems to be for von Balthasar. Is it a location of divine judgment for sin? This also needs to be answered in the affirmative. Far from trying to be dogmatic as to the precise nature of hell, von Balthasar simply seems to be balancing these two realities with one another. This balancing creates a tension. Von Balthasar believes that this tension of realities places humans "between fear and hope" with "hope" for universal salvation being described by von Balthasar as a Christian duty.[44] Von Balthasar leans heavily on the importance of hope without making little of the notion of divine punishment for sin.

Young and von Balthasar are certainly different in their assertions regarding hell. Young is far removed from any notion that hell is a punitive judgment from God whereas von Balthasar is more sympathetic to the idea. However, the hope that arises from von Balthasar's tension between divine judgment and love certainly has parallel with Young's hope for humanity. Both thinkers base their hope on God's love and the fact that God has forgiven sin in Christ. For Young, judgment is an extension of this love which seeks to heal the individual whereas von Balthasar believes judgment to be a type of inverse to hope. For Young love and judgment

40. Balthasar, *Dare We Hope*, 5.
41. Balthasar, *Dare We Hope*, 161–62.
42. Balthasar, *Dare We Hope*, 16.
43. Balthasar, *Dare We Hope*, 131.
44. Balthasar, *Dare We Hope*, 17.

are in union with one another. This does not seem to be the case, at least completely, for von Balthasar.

The parallel between Young and von Balthasar is a critical one for this discussion about Young's hopeful universalism: in von Balthasar we see what a non-dogmatic universalism may look like. Von Balthasar's work reveals the possibility that one does not need to be dogmatic about universalism in order to have hope for humanity. Furthermore, it solidifies the idea that one can have universalist tendencies but not be a dogmatic universalist. This is what we see in Young's framework. In Young, we see what a non-dogmatic form looks like with a union of divine love and judgment in view. Young certainly harmonizes divine judgment with love in a way not present in von Balthasar's framework. Yet, Young, like von Balthasar, is hopeful, not certain, of universal salvation. Young's theology of hell, therefore, is one of hope for humanity based on God's incessant love.

ENCOUNTERING YOUNG

What Young does so helpfully with his views of hell is challenge the reader to consider taking the theological concept captive to God's love. Young is not a denier of the existence of hell: he is a re-definer of the nature of hell. Hell, as with all theological concepts, must be understood using the interpretive filter of the triune God of love. All language used in Scripture to describe hell whether it's the "fiery hell" (Matt 5:22, NASB); "eternal punishment" (Matt 25:46, NIV); "the lake of fire and brimstone" (Rev 20:10, KJV); "the fiery lake of burning sulfur" (Rev 21:8, NLT); or the "second death" (Rev 20:6, KJV) must be understood and interpreted, through the lens of a God of love. Whatever the nature of hell may be, it must be an extension of this God in some way. Young seems to want his readers to come away with two main applications of this concept.

First, Young wants people to know that God never ceases to be love. The God whom Jesus revealed is unchanging and has been love since before time began and will never cease to be love even in the context of hell. Justice does not act to balance out God's love.

Hell and Hope

Likewise, God's holiness does not offer a "yeah, but . . . " to God's love. All of God's characteristics stem from, and are informed by, his love. This love does not contain any "hidden corners." It will not surprise us one day by being mean or frightening. It will never ask us to be harsh with our words, or to harm another person. Indeed, love never fails or ends (1 Cor 13:8). Young offers a possibility of how this love of God, which is never ending, can be understood considering the existence of hell. Young's devotion to using God's love as a theological filter through which we know him is admirable, and I find littledisagreement with him on this subject.

Second, Young wants us to build hope upon this understanding of love. We have all known loved ones who have died without a relationship with Christ, and we have all considered whether they "made it" in some way. We've all heard stories of people who have lost their unbelieving children or spouses in horrific ways; of civilians living in war-torn countries who have died unexpectedly from rocket fire or bombs; and of people growing up in abusive houses who turn to drugs for emotional relief only to overdose without seemingly finding peace in Christ. The list goes on and on, of course. And yet, pastorally, what is our response to those left behind? When the theological rubber meets the road of practical life, what will we say? I'm going to go out on a limb and say that I know not a single pastor who would fail to have hope when consoling a grieving parent or widow or friend. What else do we have to offer people in those situations? We don't say, "Well, we all know where they are now, so it's best to move on!" No, we encourage them to *trust* God's love. Why would we say such a thing unless, deep down, we too hoped?[45] This, however, is different in my mind

---

45. I'm not making statements that I am personally a universalist, nor that I believe in postmortem conversion. I'm in alignment with T.F. Torrance on the subject as discussed in his refutation of Robinson's article, "Universalism—Is It Heretical?," 139–55. See Torrance "Universalism or Election," 310–18. Torrance argues that God's love has been manifested fully in Christ's death, and therefore there is no "nth degree" to which this love must be manifested further as in the case of universalism, 310. This manifestation is independent of the final salvation of all humanity, 310. According to Torrance, only human logic demands that God's love be manifested in universalism, 311.

from a hope in *universal* salvation. There is a difference between consoling someone left behind and asserting that all people *can* or *will* be saved in a postmortem existence. While I believe we can console people and encourage them to trust God with their family members, this is not the same in my mind as asserting hope for *every* person as if all people will have the ability to be saved after death. This brings me to a point of disagreement with Young. My personal belief is that those in hell will not want to believe in Jesus, and that they will be so far given over to their sin that they will be in a perpetual state of being in the darkness of their sin and consequently hating God (Rom 1 and the occurrences of "weeping and gnashing of teeth" in Scripture). To be sure, this existence is not the result of God's doing. Rather, it is God's honoring of their decision to reject him. I agree with Young, however, in his rejection of the concept of divine separation in hell. I do believe, based on Rev 14 and on a general understanding of God's universal presence, as well as the idea that Christ is life and is therefore connected to all living things in some way (John 14:6), that hell is the presence of God from the perspective of an unbelieving, and consequently unregenerate, individual ("It is a dreadful thing to fall into the hands of the living God" as Heb 10:31 states, NIV). Yet, I do not believe it is only God's love that is encountered in hell by the unbeliever though to say that God ceases to love anybody is infinitely problematic. I'm convinced that hell is the experience of God as love, but also as truth itself. In this life we can distract ourselves from truth. In the afterlife, this distraction will be impossible because we will be in the full reality of God's presence. Consequently, people will be tortured by his presence because they are not compatible with his truth (Rev 14:10). This, I believe, is what causes people to solidify their hatred of him and reject him forever.

In my assessment, hope is not a bad thing at all. Sometimes hope is the avenue that God uses to heal us from the tragedy of losing friends and family members who did not know Jesus. Hope also allows us to concede that we simply do not know every corner of theology, nor do we have all the answers. Furthermore,

Hell and Hope

it recognizes the existence of certain obscure verses in Scripture which use language that could be interpreted as supporting the concept of universalism (for example, Phil 2:10–11, Rom 14:11, and the implications of the New Jerusalem's open gates in Rev 21:25). Hope arises out of a *trust* in God. Our trust is in the goodness of God, the fairness of God, and the grace of God, in every context. This seems to be what Young ultimately calls us to in our interpretation of Scripture and our journey through life. Young offers a lens through which we may understand hell, and all theological topics with which he interacts, through the lens of God's love. This is truly a gift for the believer for it dares us to leave the harbor of safety, and journey into the sea of theological inquiry into the triune God of love, the God who is unrelenting in their pursuit of creation. The love which was poured out upon the earth through the creation of humanity and spilt upon the ground at the crucifixion of Jesus. God's love pursues humanity in the midst of its struggles and afflictions, seeking to honor the decisions of God's creation while working each choice, good or bad, together for its good. This love, which can only be described as otherworldly, does not cease in its incarnational expressions in this life, nor does it back down from challenging our preconceptions of theology. It forever emanates from eternity as the Father, Son, and Spirit, ceaselessly love and seek relationship with their people. This is the heartbeat of Young's theological framework, a love in the key of three.

Appendix
Addressing James B. De Young and Common Misconceptions of Young's Theology

"The single biggest problem with communication is the illusion that it has taken place."

GEORGE BERNARD SHAW

WHEN I FIRST THOUGHT OF writing a book about Young's theology, my initial plan was to frame the entire book around what I believed to be some problematic misconceptions of what Paul Young believes arising out of the work of James B. De Young. I'd then use these misconceptions to provide an analysis to Young's beliefs in order that helpful conversation may ensue. Unfortunately, this proved to be untenable.

De Young has written two books designed as stark criticisms of Young's beliefs: *Burning Down the Shack* and *Exposing "Lies We Believe about God."* My initial plan was to go through each book and offer my own analysis of not only Young's beliefs but also those criticisms offered by De Young. However, I found the analysis present in De Young's work to be problematic for a few reasons. First, De Young, as well-meaning as he may have intended to be, did

Appendix

not offer a scholarly enough analysis of Young's beliefs. The books were largely comparisons between Young's beliefs and De Young's own theological convictions and interpretations of Scripture. To be sure, De Young was writing a more popular work. However, an analysis of Young or any theologian, regardless of the specific genre, must have a certain academic tone conducive to analysis that I simply did not find in De Young's works. I was surprised at how little De Young actually understood Young's beliefs, and how little effort seemed to be exerted to try and understand them.

Second, and related to the first, it was clear from the beginning that De Young seemed to have inserted a rather negative tone into his works. As I read them, it became more and more clear that these books were not designed to give an objective analysis of Young's works, or even a helpful criticism, but were rather an attack on not only Young but even those who appreciate him or invite him to speak at an event.[1] My conviction is that De Young's assessment of Young is largely based not on sound analysis or a desire to have objective conversation about complex theological themes, but a misunderstanding and misrepresentation of Young's beliefs and a tone which is genuinely unhelpful for theological conversation. To respond to such a book would, indeed, be a distraction from the goal of the work which was always focused on better understanding Young's beliefs and providing meaningful interaction with them. Yet, De Young's assertions regarding Young's theology are not only his own: they are shared by many readers, and non-readers, of Young. Therefore, I thought it would be helpful to frame this appendix largely around what I perceive to be misconceptions about Young's theology largely expressed by De Young. Those misconceptions chosen do not represent an exhaustive list. I specifically chose those that I felt might deserve more time than allotted in the main text of this work. My hope is that this analysis, along with this book, will allow for bridges to be built

---

1. See De Young, *Burning*, 235-36. See also De Young, *Exposing*, 220, where De Young calls theologians who sympathize with Young "religious quacks." This is an example of the type of language that is not conducive to helpful conversation.

Appendix

and conversations to be had between groups living with Jesus in their own theological corners.

MISCONCEPTION #1:
YOUNG IS A SYSTEMATIC THEOLOGIAN

Systematic theology, perhaps overly simply put, is a theological discipline in which beliefs about God or creation are demonstrated to be parts of greater systems. Often there is a central theological locus that is then demonstrated to be connected to other theological loci, or perhaps, several theological loci are demonstrated to be part of the same theological "network" of thought. Not all writers write from a systematic mindset. This changes the required approach to their material. It would be a mistake, for example, to read *Eve* and walk away believing that Young has expressed, completely, what he believes about a certain subject and has thoroughly demonstrated how the subjects covered therein are integrated with other beliefs. Young's works are not systematic presentations of truth: they are expressions of his journey and process with God. Young writes in such a way as to provoke conversation and thought about complex issues, not provide complex solutions to these issues. This is because Young loves questions and conversation. Watch any of his sermons, or read any of his books, and you will likely find yourself saying, "Yeah, but what about?" or "How does this work with?" or "What do we do with?" That's the purpose of his writing: questions and conversations, which come from his own faith, to spur people on in their relationship with God. Furthermore, Young writes largely in the fiction genre. Fiction is, inherently, more experiential in nature than it is systematic. Young's works are experiences, not systematic presentations of theology.

Any criticism of Young's works, or presentation of Young's beliefs, must take this into account. If we are to discover thematic threads in Young's writing, we ought not see these threads as comprehensive and his last word on an issue. This book, for example, has sought to lift concepts from his texts to provide explanation and interaction with them. Yet, I've done this knowing that there is

Appendix

likely much that Young believes that influences his theology that I know nothing about. This is a point that De Young, in his critiques of Young's theology, seems to have missed. De Young approaches Young's works in a more systematic manner than is helpful. For example, in *Exposing*, De Young often quotes numerous Scripture passages in order to rebuke Young's beliefs.[2] The insinuation seems to be that Young did not use an equal amount of verses during the writing of his works, and therefore is lacking in theological integrity. However, as important as Scripture is in forming our beliefs about God, this is ultimately a comparison between apples and oranges. For example, we cannot expect *The Shack* (an apple), to have a fully fleshed out theology of humanity's belonging to God as De Young seems to desire in his critiques (an orange) of Young's positions. De Young ought not expect Young's words on adoption to be comprehensive and to consider numerous scripture passages in-text.[3] This would make for truly lackluster fiction. I have little doubt that Young, if writing a non-fiction systematic theology, would cite some of the same verses as De Young uses in his critiques. Yet, this is not his goal as a writer, at least as of yet. De Young, therefore, does not seem to recognize that he is critiquing theological fiction systematically without any recognition of the differences in genre. This essentially forces Young into a theological corner in which De Young can misrepresent Young's beliefs, and then form his own supposedly comprehensive scriptural argument to critique them (straw man argumentation). This critique tries to discredit Young's process and is ultimately unhelpful for conversation. We should not expect systematic theology from Young, and our critiques of him ought to take this into consideration. That is not his contribution to the conversation about God. Rather, we should expect to see his testimony, in fiction form, and the questions he has had over the years offered to us with open hands.[4]

2. For example see De Young, *Exposing*, 4–8, where De Young cites multiple passages to disprove Young's assertion that all people are God's children.

3. De Young, *Exposing*, 4–8.

4. The "open-handed" nature of Young's argumentation is seen in every interview or sermon studied for this project.

Appendix

MISCONCEPTION #2: YOUNG IS A FALSE TEACHER

A quick search on Google reveals a plethora of articles written about Young's supposedly false teaching.[5] I've also found that while the vast majority of Christians I know love Young's work (especially *The Shack*) there are some that do insinuate that he has left true Christianity. The problem with the assertion that Young, or anybody, has left "true" teaching is that there has been non-stop debate throughout two thousand years of church history as to precisely what is true teaching, and what is not. For example, some likely find the concept of unlimited atonement, as opposed to limited atonement, to be heretical. This is because of the Reformed and Calvinist influence on the individual. If we aren't careful, our theological backgrounds prime us with a foundation from which to judge certain concepts as heretical that are, in reality, highly debatable. We certainly have a tendency to judge anything that does not belong on our own theological island.

De Young, unsurprisingly, believes that Young is a false teacher. In the preface of *Exposing*, De Young quotes Jer 23:26–28, 32; 1 Tim 4:16; 1 Tim 6:3–5; 1 Tim 6:20; 2 Tim 1:13–14; 2 Tim 3:13–17; 2 Tim 4:1–4; Titus 3:10; and Jude 24–25 to prime the reader for the false teaching they are about to encounter in Young's works.[6] The verses chosen by De Young do warn against false teaching. However, none of the verses describe beliefs held by Young. De Young is simply taking the theme of false teaching described in these verses, filtering it through his own interpretation of theological concepts, and applying it to Young's theology. This is not a practice unique to De Young. We all tend to label beliefs as "false" if we are unfamiliar with them. It's just easier than processing them with the individuals who hold them. We like systems because they organize

---

5. See Ortlund, "The god of Wm. Paul Young," https://www.thegospelcoalition.org/reviews/lies-we-believe-god-william-paul-young/. The article heavily implies that Young has deviated from orthodox Christianity into heresy. See also West, "Wm. Paul Young Teaches New Age," https://bereanresearch.org/wm-paul-young-teaches-new-age-lie-separation-tbn/.

6. De Young, *Exposing*, vi–viii.

Appendix

God in some manner. This is not a bad thing as long as we are open to having God prove us wrong and deconstruct our systems. But when we define terms such as "false teaching" or "heresy" according to our understanding of beliefs, then we set ourselves up for a very lonely and alienating existence. We will soon find that barely anyone lives on our theological island with us. Furthermore, we may even find ourselves banned from our own island one day as our preconceptions are challenged.

In response to this assertion that Young is a false teacher, I thought it would be helpful to see precisely how the New Testament defines false teaching. Then, in the end, we can determine if Young does indeed fit this mold. From what I can tell, there are nine teachings that are labelled, or heavily inferred by Scripture, as "false" in the New Testament: sin is permissible and should be celebrated; Jesus did not come in the flesh; Jesus is not the Christ; Jesus is not the Son of God; Jesus was not crucified for our sins; Jesus did not rise from the grave; Jesus is not the only way to the Father; the law and grace are compatible; and God is not one being in three persons. These teachings are "false" because those who do not believe these assertions are not viewed as being part of the Christian faith. I realize that the following criterion for false teaching is my own observation and can be subject to scrutiny. However, I've intentionally tried to keep my observations rooted in what Scripture defines as false teaching, and what Scripture overtly states as eternal truth: I've painted with very broad strokes to encourage as much conversation as possible.

A. Sin is permissible and should be celebrated

> "If we claim to have fellowship with him and yet walk in the darkness, we lie and do not live out the truth." 1 John 1:6, NIV

> "If we claim we have not sinned, we make him out to be a liar and his word is not in us." 1 John 1:10, NIV

Appendix

> "No one who has been born of God practices sin, because His seed remains in him; and he cannot sin continually, because he has been born of God." 1 John 3:9, NASB

> "For speaking loud boasts of folly, they entice by sensual passions of the flesh those who are barely escaping from those who live in error." 2 Pet 1:18, ESV

The passages in 1 John are written to a group of proto-Gnostic heretics who believed that the flesh or physical human condition was evil. Because the flesh was evil, sin could be expressed and tolerated because at death this evil body was left behind while the spirit "graduated" to the next life. John rebuked this notion even going so far as to label these figures as not being "born of God" and being without his word indwelling them. The false teachers spoken of in 2 Peter 1 shared similar characteristics. They also celebrated sin while denying Jesus (2 Pet 1: 1–3). The New Testament is clear: sin is not of God, and God desires to free his creation from bondage to sin. Those who know God have been set free from sin. Anyone who teaches the celebration of sin, is a false teacher in New Testament terms.

B. Jesus did not come in the flesh

> "For many deceivers have gone out into the world, those who do not acknowledge Jesus Christ as coming in the flesh. This is the deceiver and the antichrist." 2 John 1:7, NASB

> "That which was from the beginning, which we have heard, which we have seen with our eyes, which we looked upon and have touched with our hands, concerning the word of life— the life was made manifest, and we have seen it, and testify to it and proclaim to you the eternal life, which was with the Father and was made manifest to us— that which we have seen and heard we proclaim also to you, so that you too may have fellowship with us; and indeed our fellowship is with the Father and with his Son Jesus Christ." 1 John 1:1–3, ESV

Appendix

Here John is again addressing a belief present in proto-Gnosticism: Jesus did not actually come in the flesh. The apostle John was clear: if anyone teaches that Jesus did not come in the flesh, they are not of God and are consequently deceivers. My conviction is that this is precisely what he combats in 1 John 1 by using sensory descriptions of Jesus. John is making the point that Jesus did come in the flesh and this reality is a foundation for the faith.

C. Jesus is not the Christ

> *"Who is the liar except the one who denies that Jesus is the Christ? This is the antichrist, the one who denies the Father and the Son."* 1 John 2:22, NIV

If any individual denies, or teaches, that Jesus is not the Christ, or anointed one, then they are described as "the antichrist" and liars.

D. Jesus is not the Son of God

> *"Whoever denies the Son does not have the Father; the one who confesses the Son has the Father also."* 1 John 2:23, NASB

Jesus's sonship to the Father is also a critical theological component of the New Testament. If Christ's sonship is denied, then the entirety of his mission on earth is rendered moot. Jesus is the second person of the Trinity and reveals the very nature of the Trinity because of this (Col 1 and Heb 1).

E. Jesus did not die for our sins

> *"For I delivered to you as of first importance what I also received: that Christ died for our sins in accordance with the Scriptures, and that he was buried..."* 1 Cor 15:3-4, ESV

Appendix

> "For I determined to know nothing among you except Jesus Christ, and Him crucified." 1 Corinthians 2:2, NASB

Jesus's death is the foundation for the New Covenant. The New Covenant is made in his blood (Luke 22:20, Heb 9:16). If Jesus's death is denied, then the entirety of His salvific mission is denied. There is no forgiveness apart from his death in the New Covenant (Heb 9:16, 22; 10:10–14). Furthermore, Paul describes Christ's death as a critical component of the gospel message. There is no resurrection without the death and consequently no faith.

F. Jesus did not rise from the grave

> "For I handed down to you as of first importance what I also received, that Christ died for our sins according to the Scriptures, and that He was buried, and that He was raised on the third day according to the Scriptures..."
> 1 Cor 15:3-4, NASB

> "But if there is no resurrection of the dead, then not even Christ has been raised; and if Christ has not been raised, then our preaching is in vain, your faith also is in vain." 1 Cor 15:13-14, NASB

The resurrection of Christ is the validation of the entirety of his life. It is with the resurrection that we Christians know that we have, not a blind faith, but a living and breathing faith that is guaranteed by the person of Christ. If a teacher denies the resurrection, then he or she denies the very foundation of Christianity.

G. Jesus is not the only way to the Father

> "Jesus said to him, 'I am the way, and the truth, and the life; no one comes to the Father except through Me.'" John 14:6, NASB

> "Therefore Jesus said again, "Very truly I tell you, I am the gate for the sheep. All who have come before me are thieves

Appendix

> *and robbers, but the sheep have not listened to them. I am the gate; whoever enters through me will be saved. They will come in and go out, and find pasture. The thief comes only to steal and kill and destroy; I have come that they may have life, and have it to the full." John 10:7–10, NIV*

These two passages express the most significant reality of the Christian message: we are saved, not by intellectual musings but by a person. Jesus leads his children into the pasture where they can find freedom through relationship with himself and the entire Trinity. This imagery of the pasture is critical because it expresses a place of rest founded on the person of Christ. When I read these passages, I am reminded that we as Christians can be very wrong about so much, and still find pasture. It's for this reason that Jesus, as a person, must be viewed as the only way to the Father.

H. Law and Grace are Compatible[7]

> *"For Christ is the end of the law for righteousness to everyone who believes." Rom 10:4, ESV*

> *"It was for freedom that Christ set us free; therefore keep standing firm and do not be subject again to a yoke of slavery. Look! I, Paul, tell you that if you have yourselves circumcised, Christ will be of no benefit to you. And I testify again to every man who has himself circumcised, that he is obligated to keep the whole Law. You have been severed from Christ, you who are seeking to be justified by the Law; you have fallen from grace." Gal 5:1–4, NASB*

The Old Testament law existed to show humanity the futility of trying to make itself right with God (Rom3:19–20). This law paradigm existed until Christ arrived (Gal 3:24). The law leads us to the gospel of grace wherein we are fully reliant on God's forgiveness of our sins in Christ and not reliant on our own works. Paul called those who violated this principle "judaizers" in his

---

7. For a more in-depth study of this see my book Nelson, *Fight for Grace*, 19–36.

Appendix

letter to the Galatians. He rejected their teachings because they overtly contradicted the gospel of grace.

I. God is not one being in three persons

> *"I am no longer going to be in the world; and yet they themselves are in the world, and I am coming to You. Holy Father, keep them in Your name, the name which You have given Me, so that they may be one just as We are."* John 17:11, NASB

> *"And then a voice came from the cloud, saying, "This is My Son, My Chosen One; listen to Him!"* Luke 9:35, NASB

> *"Therefore go and make disciples of all nations, baptizing them in the name of the Father and of the Son and of the Holy Spirit..."* Matt 29:19, NIV

> *"And because we are his children, God has sent the Spirit of his Son into our hearts, prompting us to call out, 'Abba, Father.'"* Gal 4:6, NLT

A simple study of church history reveals that while past Christians unreservedly acknowledged the existence of the Trinity, it took some time for church councils to agree on definitive statements about its existence (codification). Furthermore, the New Testament does not outrightly say that "God is a Trinity." However, the triune existence of God is heavily demonstrated throughout Scripture, and the cost of deviating from this principle is always detrimental to theology. One need not look further than the theology of Jehovah's Witnesses or Latter-Day Saints to see the catastrophic consequences of rejecting the biblical, trinitarian God. Thus, if the triune existence of God is rejected in a teaching, then said teaching can be labelled as false.

The above observations in the New Testament represent what I believe to be the core characteristics of false teachings or false teachers. These are the foundations for all that makes the Christian faith so wonderful! Yet, we can disagree on the application

Appendix

of these truths. This is where conversation is so critical. As far as I can understand from his work, Young is in violation of nothing on this list. We may disagree with him in his application of these things, say the death of Christ to hopeful universalism as an example, but we do not have a biblical warrant to label him as a false teacher ("universalism" as a term isn't even mentioned in the New Testament!). We must be very slow to label people as heretics or false teachers and to do so only in order to protect those that they may hurt. So much of Christian division arises from labels, and these labels are often not about the above points but about the application of these points. We can be very wrong on something, and our wrong beliefs can have massive consequences. However, there seems to be more said of "false" teaching than "wrong" teaching in Scripture.

MISCONCEPTION #3: YOUNG IS A PLURALIST

I will not add much to the chapter written combatting this misconception, however, there is a brief section in De Young's *Burning Down the Shack* that deserves some engagement. De Young claims that Young is a pluralist because in *The Shack* "Papa reminds Mack again that he created freedom for people to choose independence if they wish, but it came at great cost–the death of Jesus to provide 'a path of reconciliation.'"[8] De Young focuses in on Young's use of the indefinite article "a" in "a path of reconciliation" and claims that this statement is an attempt by Young to present Jesus as simply one way to God.[9] He then claims that Young "elsewhere" identifies Jesus as the best way but not the only way.[10] This last statement by De Young does not contain any references to specific places where this theme apparently exists in Young's works. De Young also states that "some critics" have concluded that Young is a pluralist based on these statements, however, he also leaves out direct references

8. De Young, *Burning*, 187.
9. De Young, *Burning*, 187.
10. De Young, *Burning*, 187.

Appendix

to these critics in this section, which makes his statements difficult to analyze.

In my analysis, De Young has misrepresented the context of the statement in *The Shack*. He makes it sound as though the point of the section is to present salvation in a pluralistic context. However, in the novel, Papa is simply giving a brief overview of the condition of humanity and his decision to heal this condition through Christ. Young is clearly not making a pluralistic statement with his choice to present Jesus as "a path" instead of "the path." Reading the passage it becomes clear that "the path" would not flow as well in the sentence. Young's choice to use "a path" is much more fitting to the conversational tone of the passage–Young seems to be avoiding overly declarative language in order to gently invite people into conversation. De Young is placing far too much weight on Young's choice to use this indefinite article. *The Shack*, and Young's other writings and media present, quite conclusively, Jesus as the only way to God. It seems that De Young is genuinely proof texting Young's work with his claim.

MISCONCEPTION #4:
YOUNG IS A UNIVERSALIST

The term "universalist" is widely used today in varying contexts. Typically, as I've argued in this work, the term describes the ultimate salvation of all people. Pluralistic universalism is the belief that Jesus is not the only way, but perhaps "a" way. This form is seen in the Unitarian Universalist movement. Christian universalism, however, is the conviction that all will be saved through Christ. Young does not hesitate to claim that all people are forgiven and saved through Christ. However, Young separates the actualization of this reality from the reality itself. It is possible, in Young's theology, for God to have forgiven all people including those not in relationship with himself. It is possible for God to have saved all people even if he gives people the choice to participate in this salvation. As argued in this book, such statements are not unfamiliar to theological thinkers of the past like Barth and MacDonald.

Appendix

What Young is arguing is that salvation is achieved for all, but not everyone participates in it. Because Young avoids declarative statements about all individuals choosing Christ, Young cannot be labelled as a universalist. Only those who maintain, unabashedly, that all must be saved can be labelled as such.

De Young's assessment of Young's supposed universalism is problematic for a few reasons. First, in *Burning Down the Shack*, De Young confuses two concepts in Young's works: God's forgiveness of humanity and saving relationship with humanity. It seems that De Young believes that all who are forgiven are necessarily in relationship with God.[11] However, he addresses this without seeking to differentiate, or really to understand, the differentiation in Young's work between God's objective decision and action in Christ, and humanity's response to this action. These are equally holy sides to the same coin for Young. God has made a decisive action on behalf of humanity in Christ, however, God honors humanity's decisions.

Second, De Young labels Young's view of redemption as universal reconciliation and uses this term as a blanket label for universalism.[12] However, the term itself is confusing and not well defined by De Young in relation to other labels used to describe universalistic theology. It is completely possible to believe, as an example, that God reconciled the world to himself through Christ, and invites all to be reconciled.

> "God was in Christ reconciling the world to Himself, not imputing their trespasses to them, and has committed to us the word of reconciliation...we implore you on Christ's behalf, be reconciled to God." 2 Cor 5:19, NKJV

If, indeed, universal reconciliation is a helpful label, then it seems quite biblical: God reconciled the world in Christ, and we ought to be reconciled. Such a reality fits Young's theological paradigm: the reality of salvation, and the invitation to participate in this salvation. Perhaps, then, De Young's argument would be

---

11. De Young, *Burning*, 190.
12. De Young, *Exposing*, 105.

Appendix

strengthened by a deeper exploration not only of Young's position, but of his own theological labels.

The last point for this section is based on De Young's analysis of Young in chapter 25 of *Exposing*. This chapter is a response to chapter 13 in Young's *Lies*. In the chapter Young is criticizing the idea that salvation is the result of a non-relational marketing campaign.[13] In his experience, Christianity is often about selling Jesus to people as if he is a commodity (I can't say I disagree with his assessment). In order to combat this concept, Young declares that salvation is not based upon one's reception of the gospel through a special prayer or action. For Young, this distracts too much from the all-encompassing work of Christ.[14] For Young, the good news is that Jesus has achieved salvation for all people, not made possible the salvation of all people (an expression of the opposite of limited atonement).[15] This salvation is through God's inclusion of humanity into the life of Jesus and consequently into the life of the entire Trinity.[16] This was done, according to Young, without our say as a gift of grace.[17] Here, Young's statements are very similar to the Calvinistic view of election: God chooses individuals without their vote. However, Young applies this concept to the entirety of humanity. Based on these statements alone, Young would be seen as a universalist. However, this is not the entirety of Young's views. Young places a high view on the holiness of human volition. This is why he maintains that our place is to participate in Christ's salvation.[18] This participation is the human response to the gospel, and this response is not guaranteed according to Young.

De Young seems to misunderstand Young's position as presented in this chapter. In De Young's mind, this chapter summarizes what he has been "speaking and writing" about with regards

---

13. Young, *Lies*, 115.
14. Young, *Lies*, 116.
15. Young, *Lies*, 117.
16. Young, *Lies*, 117–18.
17. Young, *Lies*, 118.
18. Young, *Lies*, 119.

Appendix

to Young.[19] As I read these words of De Young's, I must admit that I feel for him. He is clearly passionate about this subject and feels called to combat it by writing about Young's theology. Yet, he seems to have greatly misunderstood Young's position, or at the very least, presented it only in part without a firm understanding of how Young uses terminology. The key problem with De Young's analysis is his theological label of universal reconciliation. In some sense, De Young is not wrong: Young does believe in universal reconciliation. In fact, I bet 2 Cor 5:19–20 is one of Young's favorite passages! Yet, De Young does not approach the subject in a way that recognizes the difference between being saved in Christ and participating in this salvation according to Young's works.[20] For Young, salvation is an ontological reality: it is true for all people. However, people can participate and believe, and therefore become "saved" existentially. To be sure, such language can be confusing but, at least as Young uses it, there does remain a place for faith in Jesus.

MISCONCEPTION #5: YOUNG IS AGAINST THE CHRISTIAN CHURCH

Young's emphasis on relationship over religion have led some, like De Young, to believe that Young is against the institutional church. De Young certainly believes that Young is against the institutional church, and he sees this as a real problem for Young's theology.[21] He also argues that Young is against the "religion" of Christianity.[22] These statements, taken alone, are quite accurate. What De Young does not properly assess is what Young means by these positions. De Young seems to believe that Young, in holding these convictions, is against Christian people or church buildings. Yet, nothing could be further from the truth. If you look through

19. Young, *Lies*, 149.
20. See Young, *Shack*, 149. Jesus states that the Trinity will never force relationship on anyone, and that humans are free to live independently.
21. De Young, *Burning*, 127–28, De Young, *Exposing*, 17.
22. De Young, *Exposing*, 17.

Appendix

Young's sermons and interviews you will likely find that most of them contain both people and church buildings! He also defends the value of his fellow Christians throughout his messages. In fact, he always calls them "my people" during these recordings. Young is not against people, and he is not against people gathering in church buildings: he is against religious systems because he does not believe that Jesus came to start a religion.[23] Religion, according to Young, is a ladder of sorts built to reach or understand God. Jesus, however, is the revelation of God. In other words, we need not climb a ladder to God because Jesus reveals his heart for us. Furthermore, we need not depend on religious systems or rules because we can have a relationship with God through Christ.[24] Now, this language is likely similar to what all Christians have heard in church: Young is not saying anything new here, he is simply saying it differently. He even affirms that human systems are not "inherently evil."[25] However, these religious institutions are not the end goal for God. He works in them for us, of that Young is certain. God wants relationship. This is the context in which Young rejects religion and the institutional church: they are not to replace relationship with God. If these systems are elevated too high, then they will subvert relationship.

MISCONCEPTION #6:
YOUNG BELIEVES THAT GOD IS MORE FEMALE THAN MALE

One of the interesting criticisms I hear about Young's writing is his way of portraying God as a female. I was just recently talking with a friend about *The Shack* and this was his one criticism. He felt that it was odd for Young to treat Papa as a woman. Young's depiction of Eternal Man in Eve takes this feminine imagery even further by showing him nurse Adam from his breasts. I've found that those

---

23. Young, *Lies*, 110.
24. Young, *Lies*, 111.
25. Young, *Lies*, 111.

Appendix

who take issue with Young's use of this type of imagery often forget that they're reading a work of theological fiction. As stated earlier, Young is not writing as a systematic theologian. We cannot read about Papa who is presented as a female and a male in *The Shack* and conclude that Young believes God to be both male and female, and therefore defined according to these gender identifications. Young chooses imagery to make certain points about God. The female imagery is used to express a side of God that, let's face it, we don't see explored very often in Christian theology. We call God Father (as we should) but this label does not mean that he is masculine only. Young demonstrates that God has a maternal side as well, a nurturing nature, that expresses itself in ways reflected through female actions.

De Young's chapter dedicated to this topic is a bit difficult to navigate primarily because he seems to be arguing that Young is defining God sexually, and that he only defines God through the male and female genders of humanity.[26] De Young seems to be reading Young's works as a systematic theologian, taking Young's statements about God and assuming that he is making these statements as literal expressions of church doctrine.[27] This is seen quite clearly in De Young's assertion that Young has created false images of God through depicting him as male and female (he even asserts that Young has broken the second commandment by doing so).[28] Yet, nowhere in Young's writings does he define God as male and female. His depictions of God are images designed to communicate specific truths about God. Young even argues overtly that

26. De Young, *Exposing*, 47–48.
27. De Young, *Exposing*, 48.
28. De Young, *Exposing*, 49. This is an interesting statement for it creates challenges for determining the validity of any and all depictions of God. For example, what of the numerous people who have played Christ over the years in cinema? Many of them, early on, were not actors from the Middle East. Is this a misrepresentation of Jesus? Or consider the theological interpretations existent in each of these films. What if there is an interpretation of Christ's words that is incorrect? What if when Jesus said he'd build his church on the "rock" he was not talking about Peter, yet it was portrayed as such in the movie? De Young's statements are rather radical indeed! In fact, they seem to flirt with the Islamic prohibition against artistic depictions of Muhammad.

Appendix

imagery is not intended to define God.[29] He asserts that imagery helps to express certain attributes of God.[30] He maintains that God is not more male than female, but by doing so he also argues that he is not more female than male.[31] Instead, Young is presenting God as containing both male and female qualities, while being wholly other from humanity. He is relatable and knowable, yet unrelatable and unknowable. In *The Shack*, this presentation of male and female qualities is described as metaphorical as opposed to an actual statement about God's nature.[32] Young is not saying that God is male, or female, or male and female. Rather, he is saying that God is expressed through male and female imagery. But this is not a definitive and exhaustive expression.

MISCONCEPTION #7: YOUNG DOES NOT BELIEVE IN HELL

Those who believe that Young is a universalist, in the traditional sense of the word, also affirm that he does not believe in the typical evangelical conception of hell. De Young is a good example of this. He, quite noticeably, takes issue with Young's view that hell is not separation from God.[33] Yet, there is not much helpful discourse with Young's writings in the chapter, nor with how his conceptions of judgment fit into his greater theological framework. Instead, De Young focuses on arguing that hell is separation from God and that God, including Jesus, does punish those who reject him.[34] Yet, De Young seems so focused on disproving Young that he does not consider precisely what Young is communicating in his works. De Young's strong reaction to Young's rejection of separation from God seems to assume that Young does not believe in any form of

29. Young, *Lies*, 74.
30. Young, *Lies*, 74.
31. Young, *Lies*, 74.
32. Young, *The Shack*, 93.
33. De Young, *Exposing*, 157.
34. De Young, *Exposing*, 157–59.

Appendix

hell because he rejects the notion of separation. It's as if De Young sees in Young's writings a rejection of the concept of hell. However, Young does not reject the existence of hell, as demonstrated in this work. He just does not see eternal, punitive, conscious torment of unbelievers by God, as being compatible with a God of love. This concept, according to Young, leads people into an unhealthy fear of God.[35]

For Young, hell, whatever it is, is a rejection of God's love and presence while being in the very midst of his love and presence. This definition of the term does not make hell any less torturous; it simply does not assert that God is directly torturing unbelievers. They are tortured in his presence and by his presence (much like Rev 14). The mechanism for this torture is not God, at least directly, but the sins of the individual. Therefore, Papa calls sin its "own punishment" in *The Shack*.[36] Hell is the full reality of the individual's chosen independence from God in the midst of his unabashed love for the individual. Young's language is largely reminiscent of Rom 1 which presents sin in this way (Rom 1:24, 27). According to Rom 1:24, God gave humanity over to its sinful choices and it received the punishment of these choices through the decision to sin. Young's understanding of hell presents a mechanism for the punishment which occurs in hell: sinful decisions and independence. Young absolutely leaves room for this existence in hell to last forever because of his high view of human volition.[37] In theory, someone could be tormented forever should they choose to be. Thus, Young does not reject the concept of an individual staying in hell for all eternity. He rejects the absence of God as being the mechanism for the individual's torture. Those in hell are tortured because God is there, not because he is absent (much like the view witnessed in Eastern Orthodox conceptions of hell).

35. De Young, *Exposing*, 131.
36. Young, *Shack*, 120.
37. Young, *Shack*, 136.

Appendix

MISCONCEPTION #8: YOUNG DOES NOT BELIEVE THAT CHRISTIANS ARE SINNERS

This misconception is based on Young's emphasis, seen throughout his works and messages, that humans have intrinsic value because they are made in the image of God. Humans are not totally depraved at the core of their being, a direct issue with Calvinism that Young often confronts.[38] Young maintains that because humans are made in the image of God, they are inherently good at the core of their being.[39] However, and this really is critical, Young does not view intrinsic goodness in the way that is often seen in in other religions such as New Age or Unitarianism. Often in these religions innate human goodness is asserted as a justification for ungodly behavior. This is especially prevalent in our culture today: we are who we feel we are and can behave accordingly. However, Young maintains that we are often not who we feel we are. Because we are made in God's image, any feeling or perception of ourselves that falls short of this, is not an accurate account of who we are. This "falling short" of our actual identity is sin in Young's theology.[40] And this sin can have disastrous consequences in our lives![41] So, it seems that Young is ultimately making value statements about humanity. We are not totally depraved, in a Calvinistic sense, but are made in the image of God. However, sin has blinded us to the truth of our design, and this blindness encourages sinful behavior.[42] As we've seen, Young is very clear that this sin needs to be forgiven, and that humanity needs salvation through Christ. However, salvation for Young is not from a sinful nature.[43]

38. Young, *Lies*, 34.
39. Young, *Lies*, 32–33.
40. Young, *Lies*, 228.
41. Young, *Lies*, 35.
42. Young, *Lies*, 35.
43. This is another area where Young and I disagree. While I agree with his view of the divine image in humanity, I believe that this does not negate the reality of the dead spirit existent in all people who have not received the gospel. In Christ, we are given a new spirit or heart that sets us free from sin

Appendix

De Young's analysis of Young's position seems to ignore the above scope of Young's views. De Young assumes that Young, because he rejects total depravity or any notion of a sin nature, does not value the work of Christ.[44] De Young further believes that Young is resistant to the concept that humans need to "be saved from the domination of sin."[45] However, no research conducted for this book, or for my PhD thesis about Young, reveals such a position. Young seems to have no problem acknowledging that humanity is dominated by sin and is in need of salvation. He simply begins at a different point than De Young. For Young, sin is a deception, a false "reality" (if such a thing can exist). It is a shadow to the light of God. It does not erase humanity's *imago dei* (image of God) but can and does enslave humanity. For Young, Jesus certainly takes away our sins, and sets us free from the deception caused by sin. He also reveals the truth of who we are beneath the brokenness caused by sin.[46] As we participate in him through faith, we experience our salvation. Young's position is certainly thought provoking and readers can decide whether they agree with it. However, as is so often the case in Christian theology, if we define our terms well and default to trusting the Holy Spirit in our conversation partners, we can at least find common ground that perhaps we did not know existed. So, Christians are sinners in Young's estimation. He agrees with two thousand years of church history and theology! However, for Young, this reality does not replace our innate goodness. It merely covers it up as a muddy sludge covers a bright, shining diamond.

(Ezek 36:26-27, Heb 8:10-12, Rom 6:18). Yet, this dead spirit is not a statement about our value. Rather, it is a statement about the consequences that have resulted from our independence from God.

44. De Young, *Exposing*, 38.
45. De Young, *Exposing*, 38.
46. De Young, *Exposing*, 35.

Appendix

MISCONCEPTION #9:
YOUNG DOES NOT BELIEVE IN DIVINE JUSTICE

I've often seen Christians question the theology of those who supposedly overemphasize the love and grace of God (I cannot remember the precise source, but Brennan Manning spoke of this at least once in his writings). I've encountered numerous Christians who, after I speak of God as love, always counter with "Well, yeah, but he's also holy and just" as if these are two mutually exclusive natures of God. The problem with such statements, as well intentioned as they are, is that they present God as dualistic, containing two natures. One nature is love (the nice God) and the other is justice (the Lord with a sword). I've never been convinced by these arguments. God can, ultimately, only be one nature at the core of his being: something has to influence all the other divine attributes. Otherwise, we end up with a God with multiple personality disorder. I find the argumentation presented by Young and so many others to be more convincing than the "yeah but.." arguments. When we discuss this topic, we need a starting point, and I would always prefer to begin with the love of God.

With this criticism of Young comes the conclusion that he is somehow imbalanced in his assessment of God's nature. De Young states as much in *Burning Down the Shack* when he argues that Young does not believe that God expresses wrath or vengeance.[47] Yet, chapter 11 in *The Shack* does not neglect the idea of God's wrath or justice (nor is this concept neglected in the rest of the book). Rather, it defines these concepts in light of God's love. Remember, definitions matter. Young absolutely believes in divine justice, however, justice for Young is not punitive in nature: it is designed to be restorative. Justice involves a removal of sin, but also restoration of the sinner. To be sure, Young leaves room for people to perish in their sins for eternity (their decision, not God's). This perishing is the mechanism for judgment and wrath, as opposed to the absence of God. However, this is not God's goal. Young simply challenges the concept that justice is a balancing act to God's love.

47. De Young, *Burning*, 7.

Appendix

MISCONCEPTION #10:
YOUNG IS NOT "BIBLICAL" IN HIS WRITINGS

Throughout De Young's two works, there is a motif of criticizing Young's exegetical practices (biblical interpretation). De Young always responds to his perception of Young's theology with a "biblical response."[48] As stated earlier, the problem with this approach is that Young largely writes fiction. This is not to say that there isn't theological truth in his work (this book has sought to demonstrate this reality). However, his genre does not typically allow for an overuse of verses in text. Furthermore, *Lies*, is not designed to be a thorough theological treatise. It is more of a conversation starter. It is also approachable for non-believers in a way few books are (in fact all of Young's books are this way). Young is able to present complex theological concepts in an approachable way without loading people down with an overabundance of Scripture that can potentially confuse and frustrate those unfamiliar with Christianity. That being said, in *Lies*, Young uses Scripture throughout. Here are just a few references from the book (some pages containing multiple references): 15, 34, 35, 46, 56, 60, 80, 95, 119, 120, 133, 134, 150, 151, 171, 193, 206, 215, 222, 232, and 241–48 which is comprised of numerous scriptures chronicling God's saga of redemption. In addition to these references, Young refers to numerous biblical concepts throughout the book and consults with various theologians including G.K Chesterton (156–57) and Dietrich Bonhoeffer (249–48). This is very much the same for his other works which contain often blatant references to Scripture and past theologians like C.S. Lewis in *Cross Roads*. Additionally, every message or sermon I've personally researched for this project contains Scripture. So, a "biblical" response to Young's work does not seem necessary if such a response is designed to accentuate Young's alleged unbiblical foundation.

---

48. See De Young, *Exposing*, 13, for example. This concept is also throughout *Burning Down the Shack*.

Appendix

MISCONCEPTION #11: YOUNG BELIEVES THAT GOD IS NEVER DISAPPOINTED WITH HIS CHILDREN

Young's emphasis on God's love does not leave out the possibility of God being angry or disappointed with his children, as De Young seems to claim.[49] De Young maintains that Young teaches that God is never disappointed in his children but does not seem to explore precisely what Young means in the context of his chapter. The chapter in *Lies* to which De Young refers is chapter 25. It is true that Young states that God is never disappointed in us.[50] However, he says this in the context of sharing of his own father's disappointment in him as a child,[51] and in the disappointment that arises when relational expectations are not met.[52] Young says that God is never disappointed in his children in this way because he knows exactly what to expect from them, and actively participates in life with them with eyes wide open.[53] This does not mean that God loves every decision made by his children. Young is clear: God hates sin. Sin is destructive and contrary to who he has built humanity to be. In *The Shack*, Papa even says that she gets angry with her children when they act in harmful, sinful ways.[54] Yet, here is the key difference: Young is speaking of a relational anger, a "disappointment" in actions that cause harm and pain, not a disappointment in his children themselves. Papa's anger is relational, and ultimately is an expression of her love and desire to heal her creation. So, in a sense, yes Young does believe that God is never disappointed in his creation. However, this is a value statement, not the statement of a passive deistic God who doesn't care about human action. This statement acts as a comparison, for Young, to the relational disappointment often present in life. God does not

---

49. De Young, *Exposing*, 94.
50. Young, *Lies*, 214.
51. Young, *Lies*, 210.
52. Young, *Lies*, 214.
53. Young, *Lies*, 214.
54. Young, *Shack*, 119.

Appendix

act like a human: he is able to love the person for who they are, not what they ought to be. Yet, God loves humanity so much that he is angry at its sins because of the self-destructive power behind them.

MISCONCEPTION #12: YOUNG DOES NOT BELIEVE IN THE GOD OF EVANGELICAL CHRISTIANITY

Some reading Young's works may find the God he speaks of to be foreign and a bit of an oddity. However, as this book has attempted to argue, Young's conception of God is by no means new. He worships the God of the Bible: the Father, Son, and the Spirit. Christians may not speak a similar language to Young about God, however, we can at least recognize that he isn't worshipping Buddha here. He is, quite obviously, a Christian (he may just not be our "type" of Christian). De Young ardently believes that Young worships a completely different God than the biblical God. De Young especially believes this is present in Young's account of the God that showed up to heal him from his brokenness and how this God differed from the fundamentalist Evangelical Christian conception of God.[55] However, as with all careful analysis, a recognition of context is key to understanding the intent of a text. Young is not saying that he worships a different God, or a secret God, from other Christians. He is simply saying that when God did show up to heal him, it was not the judgmental and overly critical God he had grown up with (the God of his evangelical Christianity).[56]

In many ways, Young's story is not unlike our own. We all grow up with conceptions about God, some good and some bad, and hopefully the bad are slowly shed and replaced by the truth of who God is through Bible study and relationship with the Holy Spirit. I know my own journey is similar. I grew up in a broken home where I too felt as if I was a disappointment. I lacked a

---

55. De Young, *Exposing*, 106 and Young, *Lies*, 236.
56. Young, *Lies*, 236.

Appendix

feeling of safety, security, and belonging. It was no surprise then that when I became a follower of Jesus, I transferred these feelings onto him and began wondering if he would ever be able to keep me safe and secure, and to provide an existence of belonging. It took years and years for me to abandon the wrong beliefs about God, and the only way I was able to do so was to immerse myself in the God, not of my upbringing, but of Jesus. Little by little, I trusted God's love for me, and little by little, he healed me and continues to do so to this day through the power of his grace.

Young's journey has inherent differences including differences in opinion from my own (I've cited just some in this work as I deemed it appropriate). However, we both understand the difference between the God of our imaginations and the God of Jesus Christ. It was not the God of Young's imagination that healed him: it was the God of Jesus. Young's delineation between the God of his evangelicalism and the God of Jesus is not only part of Young's testimony but is a statement about how human religion often obstructs our view of God. Young's is a journey out of religion and into relationship. That's the point he is making in his ministry. In fact, when all of Young's works are considered, the overarching theme is that there is only one God: the God of the Bible. However, our religions (such as his evangelical Christianity) and life-circumstances obscure our vision of him. It is this bad vision that God is delighted to heal.

Afterword

As of the writing of this book, I've been a Christian for twenty years. Just under half of the first decade was spent in desperate search for the love of God. Young's work, *The Shack*, gave me a massive shove in the right direction through its use of trinitarian imagery. Other authors such as Andrew Farley and Ralph Harris have done the same in different ways primarily through giving me answers to my burning questions about grace. Young, however, gave me questions to ponder. The questions which came from Young's books proved to be quite challenging to me over time. In fact, I couldn't let them go. This book has attempted to provide interaction with these questions that Young asks of us. The hope is that this interaction allows for clarity of his beliefs to be seen that true interaction with his theology may occur. Often, misunderstandings can act as a detrimental roadblock to giving sound thought to a belief system. To get to the actual beliefs, we need to first overcome these misunderstandings. My hope is that this work has helped to accomplish this. Now that our journey with Young has ended, we may objectively interact with his claims and decide for ourselves whether they belong in our understanding of God and the gospel, or not. My hope is also that in those areas of disagreement with Young, and of others like him, we keep the door open for future conversation. We have much to learn from one another, after all, and much to learn from the Spirit of Grace in our midst.

Bibliography

Athanasius. *On the Incarnation*. Translated by John Behr. Yonkers, NY: St. Vladimir's Seminary Press, 2011.
Balthasar, Hans Urs von. *Dare We Hope "That All Men Be Saved"?* Translated by Dr. David Kipp and Lothar Krauth. San Francisco: Ignatius, 2014.
Barth, Karl. *Church Dogmatics*, II.2. Edited by G.W. Bromiley and T.F. Torrance. Translated by G.W. Bromiley, et. al. Peabody, MA: Hendrickson, 2010.
Bhatti, Deborah, et al. *Talking about God in Practice: Theological Action Research and Practical Theology*. London: SCM, 2010.
Binder, Melissa. "'The Shack' Author Talks About Abuse, Adultery, and Atonement." https://www.oregonlive.com/faith/2015/05/the_shack_author_qa.html.
Burk, Denny. "Eternal Conscious Torment." In *Four Views on Hell*, edited by Stanley N. Gundry and Preston Sprinkle. Grand Rapids: Zondervan, 2016.
Calvin, John. *Institutes of the Christian Religion*. Translated by Henry Beveridge. Peabody, MA: Hendrickson, 2008.
De Young, James B. *Burning Down the Shack*. Washington: WND, 2010.
———*Exposing "Lies We Believe about God."* Abbotsford, WI: Aneko, 2018.
Elwell, Walter A, ed. *Evangelical Dictionary of Theology*. 2nd ed. Grand Rapids: Baker Academic, 2001.
Erickson, Millard J. *Christian Theology*. 3rd ed. Grand Rapids: Baker Academic, 2013.
Farley, Andrew and Tim Chalas. *The Perfect You*. Washington: Salem, 2021.
Greggs, Tom. "Christian Universalist View." In *The Extent of the Atonement*, edited by Adam J. Johnson and Stanley N. Gundry. Grand Rapids: Zondervan, 2019.
———"On the Nature, Task, and Method of Theology: A Very Methodist Account." *Journal of Systematic Theology* 20 (2018) 309—34.
Grudem, Wayne. *Systematic Theology*. Grand Rapids: Zondervan, 1994.
St. Gregory of Nazianzus. *On God and Christ*. Translated by Frederick Williams and Lionel Wickham. Yonkers, NY: St. Vladimir's Seminary Press, 2002.
Harmon, Steven R. *Every Knee Should Bow*. Lanham, MD: University Press of America, 2003.

Bibliography

Hick, John. *A Christian Theology of Religions*. Louisville: Westminster John Knox, 1995.

——— *Evil and the Love of God*. New York: Palgrave Macmillan, 2007.

——— *God Has Many Names*. Philadelphia: Westminster, 1982.

Irenaeus. *Against Heresies*. Edited by Alexander Roberts and James Donaldson. Jackson, MI: Ex Fontibus, 2015.

Jersak, Brad. "Nonviolent Identification and the Victory of Christ." In *Stricken by God?*, edited by Brad Jersak and Michael Hardin, 18–53. Grand Rapids: Eerdmans, 2007.

——— "Why I'm not a Universalist (But Sound like One): Reflections on David Bentley Hart's *That All Shall Be Saved*." *Clarion: Journal for Religion, Peace, and Justice*. https://www.clarion journal.com/clarion_journal_of_spirit/2019/09/harts-that-all-will-be-saved-i.html.

——— "Wm. Paul Young on Women, Ephesians 5:22, 1 Timothy 2:12." YouTube Video. https://www.youtube.com/watch?v=iqZQLAvgIWc.

St. John of the Cross. *The Collected Works of St. John of the Cross*. Translated by Kieran Kavanaugh and Otilio Rodriguez. Washington: ICS, 2017.

Lewis, C.S. *Mere Christianity*. New York: Harper One, 2001.

——— *The Problem of Pain*. New York: Harper One, 2001.

MacDonald, George. *The Hope of the Gospel*. Scotts Valley, CA: CreateSpace Independent, 2016.

——— *Unspoken Sermons*. Scotts Valley, CA: CreateSpace Independent Publishing, 2016.

MacDonald, Gregory. *The Evangelical Universalist*, 2nd ed. Eugene, OR: Cascade, 2012.

Manning, Brennan. *The Relentless Tenderness of Jesus*. Grand Rapids: Revell, 2004.

McGinn, Bernard. *The Essential Writings of Christian Mysticism*. New York: The Modern Library, 2006.

Mechthild of Magdeburg, "The Flowing Light of the Godhead." In *The Essential Writings of Christian Mysticism*, edited by Bernard McGinn, 202–7. New York: Random House, 2006.

Nelson, Andrew. *Fight for Grace*. Bloomington: Westbow, 2012.

Origen. *On First Principles*. Translated by G.W. Butterworth. Notre Dame, IN: Christian Classics, 2013.

Ortlund, Gavin. "The God of Wm. Paul Young." https://www.thegospelcoalition.org/reviews/lies-we-believe-god-william-paul-young/.

Parry, Robin A. "A Universalist View" in *Four Views of Hell*. Edited by Stanley N. Gundry and Preston Sprinkle. Grand Rapids: Zondervan, 2016.

Perkins, Bill. "Why 'The Shack' is Blasphemous." *Compass International*. https://compass.org/article-why-the-shack-is-blasphemous/.

Powys, David J. *Hell: A Hard Look at a Hard Question*. Eugene, OR: Wipf and Stock, 1997.

Bibliography

Reichenbach, Bruce R. "Healing View." In *The Nature of the Atonement*, edited by James Beilby and Paul R. Eddy. Downers Grove: Intervarsity Press, 2006.

Rigney, Joe. "Confronting the Problem(s) of Evil: Biblical, Philosophical, and Emotional Reactions to a Perpetual Question." *Desiring God.* https://www.desiringgod.org/articles/confronting-the-problems-of-evil.

Robinson, J.A.T. "Universalism—Is it Heretical?." *Scottish Journal of Theology* 2 (1949) 139–55.

Roth, Robert Paul. *Story and Reality.* Eugene, OR: Wipf and Stock, 1973.

Schreiner, Thomas R. "Penal Substitution View." In *The Nature of the Atonement*, edited by James Beilby and Paul R. Eddy. Downers Grove: IVP Academic, 2006.

Sutherland, Andrew. "From Satisfaction to Penal Substitution: Debt as a Determinative Concept for Atonement Theology in Anselm and Charles Hodge. *The Saint Anselm Journal* 13.1 (2017) 98—105.

Tolkien, J.R.R. *The Silmarillion.* New York: Del Rey, 2002.

Torrance, T.F. *Atonement.* Edited by Robert T. Walker. Downers Grove: IVP Academic, 2008.

———*The Christian Doctrine of God: One Being Three Persons.* London: T&T Clark, 2016.

———*Incarnation.* Edited by Robert T. Walker. Downers Grove: IVP Academic, 2008.

———"Universalism or Election." *Journal of Scottish Theology* 2 (1949) 310—18.

West, Marsha. "Wm. Paul Young Teaches New Age." https://bereanresearch.org/wm-paul-young-teaches-new-age-lie-separation-tbn/.

Wolfe, Kris. "Childhood Sexual Abuse." YouTube video. https://www.youtube.com/watch?v=yTCCsuLw-Dc.

Young, Wm. Paul. *Cross Roads.* New York: Faith Words, 2012.

———*Cross Roads Reflections.* New York: Faith Words, 2013.

———*Eve.* New York: Howard Books, 2015.

———*FGC Session* 10. YouTube video. https://www.youtube.com/watch?v=K8fl_wprdck.

———*FGC Session* 11. YouTube video. https://www.youtube.com/watch?v=vcHX1p2AJ6U.

———"I want to be more like Oprah." *Wm. Paul Young.* https://wmpaulyoung.com/i-want-to-be-more-like-oprah-watch-interview/.

———"The Killing House." *Wm. Paul Young.* http://wmpaulyoung.com/the-killing-house/.

———*Lies We Believe about God.* New York: Atria Books, 2017.

———*The Shack.* Los Angeles: Windblown Media, 2007.

———*The Shack Reflections.* Los Angeles: Windblown Media, 2012.

———"You Never Need to Feel Shame." *Wm. Paul Young.* https://wmpaulyoung.com/feel-shame/.

www.ingramcontent.com/pod-product-compliance
Lightning Source LLC
Chambersburg PA
CBHW072152160426
43197CB00012B/2355